MATLAB Matrix Algebra

César Pérez López

Apress®

MATLAB Matrix Algebra

Copyright © 2014 by César Pérez López

ISBN-13 (pbk): 978-1-4842-0308-8

ISBN-13 (electronic): 978-1-4842-0307-1

Managing Director: Welmoed Spahr
Lead Editor: Dominic Shakeshaft
Editorial Board: Steve Anglin, Mark Beckner, Ewan Buckingham, Gary Cornell, Louise Corrigan, Jim DeWolf, Jonathan Gennick, Robert Hutchinson, Michelle Lowman, James Markham, Matthew Moodie, Jeff Olson, Jeffrey Pepper, Douglas Pundick, Ben Renow-Clarke, Dominic Shakeshaft, Gwenan Spearing, Matt Wade, Steve Weiss
Coordinating Editor: Jill Balzano
Copy Editor: Barnaby Sheppard
Compositor: SPi Global
Indexer: SPi Global
Artist: SPi Global
Cover Designer: Anna Ishchenko

Distributed to the book trade worldwide by Springer Science+Business Media New York, 233 Spring Street, 6th Floor, New York, NY 10013. Phone 1-800-SPRINGER, fax (201) 348-4505, e-mail orders-ny@springer-sbm.com, or visit www.springeronline.com Apress Media, LLC is a California LLC and the sole member (owner) is Springer Science + Business Media Finance Inc (SSBM Finance Inc). SSBM Finance Inc is a Delaware corporation.

For information on translations, please e-mail rights@apress.com, or visit www.apress.com.

Apress and friends of ED books may be purchased in bulk for academic, corporate, or promotional use. eBook versions and licenses are also available for most titles. For more information, reference our Special Bulk Sales–eBook Licensing web page at www.apress.com/bulk-sales.

Any source code or other supplementary material referenced by the author in this text is available to readers at www.apress.com. For detailed information about how to locate your book's source code, go to www.apress.com/source-code/.

Contents at a Glance

Contents

About the Author

César Pérez López is a Professor at the Department of Statistics and Operations Research at the University of Madrid. César is also a Mathematician and Economist at the National Statistics Institute (INE) in Madrid, a body which belongs to the Superior Systems and Information Technology Department of the Spanish Government. César also currently works at the Institute for Fiscal Studies in Madrid.

Coming Soon

- *MATLAB Programming for Numerical Analysis,* 978-1-4842-0296-8
- *MATLAB Differential Equations,* 978-1-4842-0311-8
- *MATLAB Control Systems Engineering,* 978-1-4842-0290-6
- *MATLAB Linear Algebra,* 978-1-4842-0323-1
- *MATLAB Differential and Integral Calculus,* 978-1-4842-0305-7

CHAPTER 1

Matrix and Vector Variables (Numeric and Symbolic)

1.1 Variables

The concept of variable, like the concept of function, is essential when working with mathematical software. Obviously, the theoretical concept of a mathematical variable is fixed and independent of the software package, but how to implement and manage variables is very characteristic of each particular program. MATLAB allows you to define and manage variables, and store them in files, in a very simple way.

When extensive calculations are performed, it is convenient to give names to intermediate results. Each intermediate result is assigned to a variable to make it easier to use. For example, we can define the variable x and assign the value 5 to it in the following way:

>> x = 5

x =

   5

From now on, whenever the variable x appears it will be replaced by the value 5, and it will not change its value until it is redefined.

>> x ^ 2

ans =

   25

The variable x will not change until we explicitly assign another value to it.

>> x = 7 + 4

x =

   11

From this moment on, the variable x will take the value *11*.

It is very important to stress that the value assigned to a variable will remain fixed until it is expressly changed or if the current MATLAB session is closed. It is common to forget the definitions given to variables during a MATLAB session, causing misleading errors when the variables are used later in the session. For this reason, it is convenient to be able to remove the assignment of a value to a variable. This operation is performed by using the command *clear*. It is also useful to recall the variables we have defined in the present session, which is done using the command *who*:

- **The expression $x = value$ assigns the value *value* to the variable x.**

- **The command *clear* removes the value assigned to all variables.**

- **The command *clear x* removes the value assigned to the variable x.**

- **The command *clear x y* removes the value assigned to the variables x and y.**

- **The command *who* gives the names of all variables currently in memory (variables in the workspace).**

- **The command *whos* gives the names, sizes, number of items, bytes occupied, and type of all variables currently in memory.**

Here are some examples that use the variable handling commands defined above:

```
>> x = 7, y = 4 + i, z = sqrt (3)

x =

    7

y =

   4.0000 + 1.0000i

z =

   1.7321

>> p=x+y+z

p =

   12.7321 + 1.0000i

>> who

Your variables are:

ans        p        x        y        z

>> whos
```

Name	Size	Elements	Bytes	Density	Complex
ANS	1 by 1	1	8	Full	No
p	1 by 1	1	16	Full	Yes
x	1 by 1	1	8	Full	No
y	1 by 1	1	16	Full	Yes
z	1 by 1	1	8	Full	No

Grand total is 5 elements using 56 bytes

2

Now we are going to change the value of the variable y, and delete the variable x.

```
>> y = pi
```

y =

    3.1416

```
>> clear x;
>> whos
```

	Name Size	Elements	Bytes	Density	Complex
ANS	1 by 1	1	8	Full	No
p	1 by 1	1	16	Full	Yes
y	1 by 1	1	8	Full	No
z	1 by 1	1	8	Full	No

Grand total is 4 elements using 40 bytes

We see that the variable x has disappeared and that the variable y has the new value assigned, but the variable p has not changed, despite having changed two of its components. ***For an expression that contains a variable whose value has been changed, to update its value it is necessary to rerun it:***

```
>> p=y+z
```

p =

    4.8736

```
>> whos
```

	Name Size	Elements	Bytes	Density	Complex
ANS	1 by 1	1	8	Full	No
p	1 by 1	1	8	Full	No
y	1 by 1	1	8	Full	No
z	1 by 1	1	8	Full	No

Grand total is 4 elements using 32 bytes

Now all values are updated, including that of p.

As for the names that can be given to the variables, the only restriction is that they cannot start with a number or contain punctuation characters that are assigned a special meaning in MATLAB. It is also advisable to name variables with words that begin with lowercase letters, and in general with words completely in lowercase. This avoids collisions with MATLAB functions beginning with an uppercase letter. MATLAB is case sensitive. There can be any number of characters in the name of a variable, but MATLAB will handle only the first 19.

1.2 Variables and Special Constants

In many kinds of calculations we need to work with variables and special constants that the program has enabled. Here are some examples:

PI or maple ('PI'): 3.1415926535897…

i or j or maple('i'): imaginary unit (square root of - 1).

inf or maple('infinity') : Infinity, returned for example when presented with 1/0.

NaN (*Not a Number*): Indeterminate, returned for example when presented with 0/0.

realmin: the smallest usable positive real number.

realmax: the greatest usable positive real number.

finite(x): returns 1 if x is finite and zero otherwise.

isinf(x): returns 1 if x is infinity or - infinity, and zero otherwise.

isNaN(x): returns 1 if x is undetermined and zero otherwise.

isfinite(x): returns 1 if x is finite and zero otherwise.

ana: automatically creates a variable to represent the last unmapped processing result which has not been assigned to a variable.

eps: returns the distance from 1.0 to the next largest double-precision number. This is the default tolerance for floating-point operations (floating point relative accuracy). In current IEEE machines its value is 2 ^(-52).

isieee: returns 1 if the machine is IEEE and 0 otherwise.

computer: returns the type of the computer.

flops: returns the number of floating point operations that have been executed in a session (flops(0) resets the operations counter).

version: returns the current version of MATLAB.

why: returns a concise message.

cputime: returns CPU time in seconds used by MATLAB since the beginning of the session.

clock: returns a list consisting of the following 6 items: [year month day hour minutes seconds].

date: returns the current calendar date.

etime: returns the time elapsed between two *clock* type lists (defined above).

tic: enables a temporary counter in seconds that ends with the use of the variable *toc*.

toc: returns the elapsed time in seconds since the variable *tic* was activated.

LastErr: returns the last error message.

See: gives information about the program and its *Toolbox*.

Info: provides information about MATLAB.

subscribe to: gives information about the subscription to MATLAB.

whatsnew: provides information about new undocumented MATLAB features.

Here are some examples:

First we check if our computer is an IEEE machine, what type of computer it is, and find the current date and time:

```
>> isieee
```

ans =

1

```
>> computer
```

ans =

PCWIN

```
>> clock
```

ans =

1.0e + 003 *

1.9950 0.0110 0.0140 0.0100 0.0150 0.0079

```
>> date
```

ans =

14-mar-99

Now we check the CPU time (in seconds) that has passed since the beginning of the MATLAB session, as well as the number of floating-point operations that have occurred during that time:

```
>> cputime
```

ans =

23.5100

```
>> flops
```

ans =

1180

EXERCISE 1-1

Calculate the time in seconds that the computer takes to return the irrational number π to 50 decimal places.

```
>> tic; vpa 'pi' 50; toc
```

elapsed_time =

   0.110000000000001

EXERCISE 1-2

Calculate the number of floating-point operations required to calculate the numerical value of the square root of the irrational number π to default accuracy. Consider the number π first as a numerical constant, and secondly, as a symbolic constant.

```
>> flops(0);numeric((pi)^(1/2));flops
```

ans =

   427

```
>> flops(0);numeric('(pi)^(1/2)');flops
```

ans =

   6

We see that much fewer floating-point operations are required when we consider π as a symbolic constant. The calculations are faster when we work in the symbolic field.

1.3 Symbolic and Numeric Variables

MATLAB deems as symbolic any algebraic expression whose variables have previously been defined as symbolic via the command ***syms***. For example, if we want to treat as symbolic the expression $6ab + 3a^2 + 2ab$ in order to simplify it, we need to declare the two variables a and b as symbolic as shown below:

```
>> syms a b
>> simplify(6*a*b + 3*a^2 + 2*a*b)
```

ans =

*8 * a * b + 3 * a ^ 2*

The command *sym* can be used to transform a numeric expression into a symbolic expression. For example, if we want to simplify the numeric expression $2/5 + 6/10 + 8/20$, we first need to transform it into a symbolic expression via *sym(2/5+6/10+8/20)*, making the simplification as follows:

```
>> simplify (sym(2/5+6/10+8/20))
```

ans =

7/5

The variables contained in a symbolic expressions must be symbolic. Some commands for working with symbolic and numerical variables are described below:

syms x y z... t: makes the variables *x, y, z,..., t* symbolic.

syms x y z... t real: makes the variables *x, y, z,..., t* symbolic with real values.

syms x y z... t unreal: makes the variables *x, y, z,..., t* symbolic with non-real values.

syms: lists the symbolic variables in the workspace.

x = sym ('x'): *x* becomes a symbolic variable (equivalent to *syms x*).

x = sym ('x', real): *x* becomes a real symbolic variable.

x = sym('x',unreal): *x* becomes a symbolic non-real variable.

S = sym(A): creates a symbolic variable S from A, where A can be a string, a scalar, an array, a numeric expression, etc.

S = sym(A, 'option'): converts the array, scalar or numeric expression A to a symbolic variable S according to the specified option. The option can be 'f' for floating point, 'r' for rational, 'e' for error format and 'd' for decimal.

numeric(x): makes the variable or expression *x* numeric with double precision.

sym2poly(*poly*): converts the symbolic polynomial *poly* to a vector whose components are its coefficients.

poly2sym(vector): creates a symbolic polynomial whose coefficients are the components of the vector.

poly2sym(vector, 'v'): converts a symbolic polynomial in the variable *v* whose coefficients are the components of the vector.

digits(d): gives symbolic variables to an accuracy of *d* significant figures.

digits: returns the current accuracy for symbolic variables.

vpa(expr): returns the numerical result of the expression to an accuracy determined by *digits*.

vpa(expr, n): returns the numerical result of the expression to *n* significant figures.

vpa('expr', n): returns the numerical result of the expression to *n* significant figures.

pretty(expr): returns the symbolic expression in the form of standard mathematical script.

EXERCISE 1-3

Solve the equation $ax^2 + bx + c = 0$ assuming that the variable is x. Solve it when the variables are a, b or c, respectively.

Since by default MATLAB considers x to be the only symbolic variable, to solve the equation in x we don't need to declare x as symbolic. We simply use the command *solve* as follows:

```
>> solve('a*x^2+b*x+c=0')
```

ans =

```
[1/2/a*(-b+(b^2-4*a*c)^(1/2))]
[1/2/a*(-b-(b^2-4*a*c)^(1/2))]
```

But to solve the equation with respect to the variables a, b or c respectively, it is necessary to first specify them as symbolic variables:

```
>> syms a
>> solve('a*x^2+b*x+c=0',a)
```

ans =

```
-(b*x+c)/x^2
```

```
>> syms b
>> solve('a*x^2+b*x+c=0',b)
```

ans =

```
-(a*x^2+c)/x
```

```
>> syms c
>> solve('a*x^2+b*x+c=0',c)
```

ans =

```
-a * x ^ 2-b * x
```

EXERCISE 1-4

Find the roots of the polynomial $x^4 - 8x^2 + 16 = 0$ obtaining the result to default accuracy, to 20 significant figures and with double-precision. Also generate the vector of coefficients associated with the polynomial.

```
>> p = solve('x^4-8*x^2-16=0')

p =

[ 2*(2^(1/2)+1)^(1/2)]
[-2*(2^(1/2)+1)^(1/2)]
[ 2*(1-2^(1/2))^(1/2)]
[-2*(1-2^(1/2))^(1/2)]

>> vpa(p)

ans =

[    3.1075479480600746146883179061262]
[   -3.1075479480600746146883179061262]
[   1.2871885058111652494708868748364*i]
[  -1.2871885058111652494708868748364*i]

>> numeric(p)

ans =

   3.1075
  -3.1075
        0 + 1.2872i
        0 - 1.2872i

>> vpa(p,20)

ans =

[    3.1075479480600746146]
[   -3.1075479480600746146]
[  1.2871885058111652495*i]
[ -1.2871885058111652495*i]

>> syms x
>> sym2poly(x^4-8*x^2-16)

ans =

    1   0   -8   0   -16
```

EXERCISE 1-5

Find the numerical value to default precision of the abscissa of the intersection point in the first quadrant of the curves $y = \sin(x)$ and $y = \cos(x)$. Find the symbolic solution. Find the abscissa to 12 significant figures.

```
>> p = numeric(solve ('sin(x) = cos(x)'))
```

p =

    0.7854

```
>> q = sym(p)
```

q =

PI/4

```
>> digits(12);r = numeric(solve('sin(x)=cos(x)'))
```

r =

.785398163398

EXERCISE 1-6

Simplify the following expressions as much as possible:

1 / 2m - 1 / 3m + 1 / 4 m + 1 / 5m + 1 / 6m

1/2 - 1/3 + 1/4 + 1/5 + 1/6

```
>> syms m
>> simplify(1/(2*m) - 1/(3*m) + 1/(4*m) + 1/(5*m) + 1/(6*m))
```

ans =

47/60m

```
>> pretty(simplify(1/(2*m) - 1/(3*m) + 1/(4*m) + 1/(5*m) + 1/(6*m)))
```

```
 47
---
60m
```
```
>> sym(1/2 - 1/3 + 1/4 + 1/5 + 1/6)
```

ans =

47/60

1.4 Vector Variables

A variable that represents a vector of length n can be defined in MATLAB in the following ways:

```
variable = [e1, e2, e3,..., en]
variable = [e1 e2 e3... en]
```

Therefore, to define a vector variable, simply insert the vector elements between brackets separated by commas or blank spaces.

When you apply most MATLAB commands and functions to a vector variable, the result obtained is that found by applying the command or function to each element of the vector:

```
>> vector1 = [1,3,5,2.3,1/2]
```

vector1 =

   1.0000 3.0000 5.0000 2.3000 0.5000

```
>> sin(vector1)
```

ans =

   0.8415 0.1411 - 0.9589 0.7457 0.4794

```
>> exp(vector1)
```

ans =

   2.7183 20.0855 148.4132 9.9742 1.6487

```
>> log(vector1)
```

ans =

   0 1.0986 1.6094 0.8329 - 0.6931

There are different ways of defining a vector variable without explicitly bracketing all its elements, separated by commas or blank spaces.

> **variable = [first_element:last_element]: Defines the vector whose first and last elements are specified, and the intermediate elements differ by one unit.**

> **variable = [first_element:increase:last_element]: Defines the vector whose first and last elements are specified, and the intermediate elements differ by the amount specified by the increase.**

> **variable = linspace (first_element, last_element, n): Defines the vector whose first and last elements are specified, and which has in total n evenly spaced elements.**

> **variable = logspace (a,b,n): Defines the vector whose first and last elements are 10^a and 10^b, and which has in total n evenly logarithmically spaced elements.**

Here are some examples:

```
>> vector2 = [0:5:20]
```

vector2 =

    0 5 10 15 20

We have obtained the numbers between 0 and 20 separated by 5 units.

```
>> vector3 = [0:20]
```

vector3 =

  Columns 1 through 12

    0   1   2   3   4   5   6   7   8   9   10   11

  Columns 13 through 21

    12 13 14 15 16 17 18 19 20

We have obtained the numbers between 0 and 20 separated by units.

```
>> vector4 = linspace(0,10,11)
```

Vector4 =

    0   1   2   3   4   5   6   7   8   9   10

We have obtained the numbers between 0 and 10 separated by units.

```
>> vector5 = linspace (0,20,6)
```

vector5 =

    0 4 8 12 16 20

We have obtained 6 equally spaced numbers between 0 and 20.

```
>> vector6 = logspace (0,2,6)
```

vector6 =

    1.0000 2.5119 6.3096 15.8489 39.8107 100.0000

We have obtained 6 evenly logarithmically spaced numbers between 10^0 and 10^2.

We can also consider row and column vectors in MATLAB. A column vector is obtained by separating its elements by semicolons, or by transposing a row vector using a single apostrophe at the end of its definition.

```
>> a = [1;2;3;4]
```

a =

```
    1
    2
    3
    4
```

```
>> a = [1:4];b=a'
```

b =

```
    1
    2
    3
    4
```

```
>> c = (a')'
```

c =

```
    1 2 3 4
```

You can also select an element of a vector or a subset of elements.

> **x(n): returns the n-th element of the vector x.**
>
> **x(a:b): returns the a-th through b-th elements of the vector x, both inclusive.**
>
> **x(a:p:b): returns the a-th through b-th elements of the vector x, both inclusive, each separated from the next by p units (a < b).**
>
> **x(b:-p:a): returns the b-th through a-th elements of the vector x, both inclusive, each separated from the next by p units and starting with the b-th (b > a).**

Here are some examples:

```
>> x = (1:10)
```

x =

```
    1     2     3     4     5     6     7     8     9    10
```

```
>> x(6)
```

ans =

```
    6
```

We have obtained the sixth element of the vector x.

>> x(4:7)

ans =

   4 5 6 7

We have obtained the elements of the vector x located between the fourth and the seventh elements, both inclusive.

>> x(2:3:9)

ans =

   2 5 8

We have obtained the elements of the vector x located between the second and ninth elements, both inclusive, but separated from each other by three units.

>> x(9:-3:2)

ans =

   9 6 3

We have obtained the elements of the vector x located between the ninth and second elements, both inclusive, but separated from each other by three units and starting at the ninth.

Simple mathematical operations between scalars and vectors scale each element of the vector according to the defined operation, and simple operations between vectors are performed elementwise.

Below is a summary of these operations:

a = {a1, a2,..., an}, b = {b1, b2,..., bn}, c = scalar

a + c = [a1 + c, a2 + c,..., an + c]: sum of a scalar and a vector

a * c = [a1 * c, a2 * c,..., an * c]: product of a scalar and a vector

a + b = [a1 + b1, a2 + b2,... an + bn]: sum of two vectors

a.* b = [a1 * b1, a2 * b2,... , an * bn]: product of two vectors

a. / b = [a1/b1 a2/b2... an/bn]: right ratio of two vectors

a. \ b = [a1\b1 a2\b2... an\bn]: left ratio of two vectors

a. ^ c = [a1 ^ c, a2 ^ c,..., an ^ c]: scalar power of a vector

c. ^ a = [c ^ a1, c ^ a2,... ,c ^ an]: vector power of a scalar

a. ^ b = [a1 ^ b1, a2 ^ b2,... ,an ^ bn]: vector power of a vector

It must be borne in mind that the vectors must be of the same length, and that in the product, quotient, and power the first operand is followed by a point.

On the other hand, you can also set the vector variables to be symbolic using the command *syms*.

```
>> syms t
>> A=sym([sin(t),cos(t)])
```

A =

[sin (t), cos (t)]

EXERCISE 1-7

Given the vector variables a = [π, 2π, 3π, 4π, 5π] and b = [e, 2e, 3e, 4e, 5e] calculate c = sin (a) + b, d = cos (a), e = ln (b), f = c * d, g = c/d, h = d ^ 2, i = d ^ 2-e ^ 2 and j = 3d ^ 3-2e ^ 2.

```
>> a = [pi, 2 * pi, 3 * pi, 4 * pi, 5 * pi], b = [exp (1), 2 * exp (1), 3 * exp (1), 4 * exp (1),
5 * exp (1)], c=sin(a)+b, d=cos(a), e=log(b), f=c.*d, g=c./d, h=d.^2, i=d.^2-e.^2, j = 3 * d.
^ 3-2 * e ^ 2
```

a =

    3.1416 6.2832 9.4248 12.5664 15.7080

b =

    2.7183 5.4366 8.1548 10.8731 13.5914

c =

    2.7183 5.4366 8.1548 10.8731 13.5914

d =

    -1   1   -1   1   -1
e =

    1.0000 1.6931 2.0986 2.3863 2.6094

f =

    -2.7183 5.4366 - 8.1548 10.8731 - 13.5914

g =

    -2.7183 5.4366 - 8.1548 10.8731 - 13.5914

h =

    1   1   1   1   1

i =

0 - 1.8667 - 3.4042 - 4.6944 - 5.8092

j =

  -5.0000 - 2.7335 - 11.8083 - 8.3888 - 16.6183

1.5 Matrix Variables

MATLAB defines arrays by inserting in brackets all its row vectors separated by a semicolon. Vectors can be entered by separating their components by spaces or by commas, as we already know. For example, a 3 × 3 matrix variable can be entered in the following two ways:

$M = [a_{11}\ a_{12}\ a_{13};\ \ a_{21}\ a_{22}\ a_{23};\ \ a_{31}\ a_{32}\ a_{33}]$
$M = [a_{11}, a_{12}\ , a_{13}; a_{21}\ , a_{22}\ , a_{23}; a_{31}, a_{32}, a_{33}]$

Similarly we can define an array of variable dimension *(M×N)*. Once a matrix variable has been defined, MATLAB enables many ways to insert, extract, renumber, and generally manipulate its elements. The following table shows different ways to define matrix variables.

A(m,n)	*Defines the (m, n)-th element of the matrix A (row m and column n).*
A(a:b,c:d)	*Defines the subarray of A formed between the a-th and the b-th rows and between the c-th and the d-th columns, inclusive.*
A(a:p:b,c:q:d)	*Defines the subarray of A formed by every p-th row between the a-th and the b-th rows, inclusive, and every q-th column between the c-th and the d-th columns, inclusive.*
A([a b],[c d])	*Defines the subarray of A formed by the intersection of the a-th through b-th rows and c-th through d-th columns, inclusive.*
A([a b c...],[e f g...])	*Defines the subarray of A formed by the intersection of rows a, b, c,...and columns e, f, g,...*
A(:,c:d)	*Defines the subarray of A formed by all the rows in A and the c-th through to the d-th columns.*
A(:,[c d e...])	*Defines the subarray of A formed by all the rows in A and columns c, d, e,...*
A(a:b,:)	*Defines the subarray of A formed by all the columns in A and the a-th through to the b-th rows.*
A([a b c...],:)	*Defines the subarray of A formed by all the columns in A and rows a, b, c,...*
A(a,:)	*Defines the a-th row of the matrix A.*
A(:,b)	*Defines the b-th column of the matrix A.*
A(:)	*Defines a column vector whose elements are the columns of A placed in order below each other.*
A(:,:)	*This is equivalent to the entire matrix A.*
[A, B, C,...]	*Defines the matrix formed by the matrices A, B, C,...*
$S_A = [\ ]$	*Clears the subarray of the matrix A, SA, and returns the remainder.*

(continued)

diag (v)	*Creates a diagonal matrix with the vector v in the diagonal.*
diag (A)	*Extracts the diagonal of the matrix as a column vector.*
eye (n)	*Creates the identity matrix of order n.*
eye (m, n)	*Creates an m×n matrix with ones on the main diagonal and zeros elsewhere.*
zeros (m, n)	*Creates the zero matrix of order m×n.*
ones (m, n)	*Creates the matrix of order m×n with all its elements equal to 1.*
rand (m, n)	*Creates a uniform random matrix of order m×n.*
randn (m, n)	*Creates a normal random matrix of order m×n.*
flipud (A)	*Returns the matrix whose rows are those of A but placed in reverse order (from top to bottom).*
fliplr (A)	*Returns the matrix whose columns are those of A but placed in reverse order (from left to right).*
rot90 (A)	*Rotates the matrix A counterclockwise by 90 degrees.*
reshape(A,m,n)	*Returns an m×n matrix formed by taking consecutive entries of A by columns.*
size (A)	*Returns the order (size) of the matrix A.*
find (cond$_A$)	*Returns all A items that meet a given condition.*
length (v)	*Returns the length of the vector v.*
tril (A)	*Returns the lower triangular part of the matrix A.*
triu (A)	*Returns the upper triangular part of the matrix A.*
A'	*Returns the transpose of the matrix A.*
Inv (A)	*Returns the inverse of the matrix A.*

Here are some examples:

We consider first the *2 × 3* matrix whose rows are the first six consecutive odd numbers:

```
>> A = [1 3 5; 7 9 11]
```

A =

```
1 3 5
7 9 11
```

Now we are going to change the *(2,3)-th* element, i.e. the last element of *A*, to zero:

```
>> A(2,3) = 0
```

A =

```
1 3 5
7 9 0
```

We now define the matrix B to be the transpose of A:

```
>> B = A'

B =

1 7
3 9
5 0
```

We now construct a matrix C, formed by attaching the identity matrix of order 3 to the right of the matrix B:

```
>> C = [B eye (3)]

C =

1    7    1    0    0
3    9    0    1    0
5    0    0    0    1
```

We are going to build a matrix D by extracting the odd columns of the matrix C, a matrix E formed by taking the intersection of the first two rows of C and its third and fifth columns, and a matrix F formed by taking the intersection of the first two rows and the last three columns of the matrix C:

```
>> D = C(:,1:2:5)

D =

1 1 0
3 0 0
5 0 1
```

```
>> E = C([1 2],[3 5])

E =

1 0
0 0
```

```
>> F = C([1 2],3:5)

F =

1 0 0
0 1 0
```

Now we build the diagonal matrix G such that the elements of the main diagonal are the same as those of the main diagonal of D:

```
>> G = diag(diag(D))

G =

1 0 0
0 0 0
0 0 1
```

We then build the matrix H, formed by taking the intersection of the first and third rows of C and its second, third and fifth columns:

```
>> H = C([1 3],[2 3 5])

H =

7 1 0
0 0 1
```

Now we build an array I formed by the identity matrix of order 5×4, appending the zero matrix of the same order to its right and to the right of that, the unit matrix, again of the same order. Then we extract the first row of I and, finally, form the matrix J comprising the odd rows and even columns of I and calculate its order (size).

```
>> I = [eye(5,4) zeros(5,4) ones(5,4)]

ans =

1   0   0   0   0   0   0   0   1   1   1   1
0   1   0   0   0   0   0   0   1   1   1   1
0   0   1   0   0   0   0   0   1   1   1   1
0   0   0   1   0   0   0   0   1   1   1   1
0   0   0   0   0   0   0   0   1   1   1   1

>> I(1,:)

ans =

1   0   0   0   0   0   0   0   1   1   1   1

>> J = I(1:2:5,2:2:12)

J =

0   0   0   0   1   1
0   0   0   0   1   1
0   0   0   0   1   1

>> size(J)

ans =

3 6
```

19

We now construct a random matrix K of order 3×4, reverse the order of the rows of K, reverse the order of the columns of K and then perform both operations simultaneously. Finally, we find the matrix L of order 4×3 whose columns are obtained by taking the elements of K sequentially by columns.

```
>> K = rand(3,4)

K =

    0.5269    0.4160    0.7622    0.7361
    0.0920    0.7012    0.2625    0.3282
    0.6539    0.9103    0.0475    0.6326

>> K(3:-1:1,:)

ans =

    0.6539    0.9103    0.0475    0.6326
    0.0920    0.7012    0.2625    0.3282
    0.5269    0.4160    0.7622    0.7361

>> K(:,4:-1:1)

ans =

    0.7361    0.7622    0.4160    0.5269
    0.3282    0.2625    0.7012    0.0920
    0.6326    0.0475    0.9103    0.6539

>> K(3:-1:1,4:-1:1)

ans =

    0.6326    0.0475    0.9103    0.6539
    0.3282    0.2625    0.7012    0.0920
    0.7361    0.7622    0.4160    0.5269

>> L = reshape(K,4,3)

L =

    0.5269 0.7012 0.0475
    0.0920 0.9103 0.7361
    0.6539 0.7622 0.3282
    0.4160 0.2625 0.6326
```

EXERCISE 1-8

Given the square matrix of order 3 whose entries are the first nine natural numbers, find its inverse, its transpose and its diagonal. Transform it into a lower triangular matrix and an upper triangular matrix and rotate it by 90 degrees counterclockwise. Find the sum of the elements in the first row and the sum of the diagonal elements. Extract the subarray whose diagonal is formed by the elements at $_{11}$ and $_{22}$ and also remove the subarray whose diagonal elements are at $_{11}$ and $_{33}$.

```
>> M = [1,2,3;4,5,6;7,8,9]
```

M =

     1   2   3
     4   5   6
     7   8   9

```
>> A = inv(M)
```

Warning: Matrix is close to singular or badly scaled.

Results may be inaccurate. RCOND = 2.937385e-018

A =

  1.0e + 016 *

    0.3152 - 0.6304   0.3152
   -0.6304   1.2609 - 0.6304
    0.3152 - 0.6304   0.3152

```
>> B = M'
```

B =

     1 4 7
     2 5 8
     3 6 9

```
>> V = diag(M)
```

V =

     1
     5
     9

```
>> TI = tril(M)
```

TI =

```
    1    0    0
    4    5    0
    7    8    9
```

```
>> TS = triu(M)
```

TS =

```
    1    2    3
    0    5    6
    0    0    9
```

```
>> TR = rot90(M)
```

TR =

```
    3    6    9
    2    5    8
    1    4    7
```

```
>> s = M(1,1)+M(1,2)+M(1,3)
```

s =

```
    6
```

```
>> sd = M(1,1)+M(2,2)+M(3,3)
```

sd =

```
    15
```

```
>> SM = M(1:2,1:2)
```

SM =

```
    1    2
    4    5
```

```
>> SM1 = M([1 3],[1 3])
```

SM1 =

```
    1    3
    7    9
```

The most important matrix operations are summarized below:

A + B, A - B, A * B: addition, subtraction and product of matrices

$A\backslash B = inv(A) * B$ if A it is square.

$A\backslash B$ is the solution of the system $AX = B$ in the sense of least-squares if A it is not square

B coincides with $(A \,'\!\backslash B')'$

A^n coincides with $A * A * A * \ldots * A^n$ n times (n scalar)

p^A performs the calculation only if p is a scalar

Here are some examples:

```
>> A = [1, 3, 5; pi exp(pi) sin(1); i 2 * i 1 + i]
```

A =

```
  1.0000    3.0000   5.0000
  3.1416    2.7183   0.0000
  1.0000i   2.0000i  1.0000 + 1.0000i
```

We have defined a complex matrix. Next we will calculate its inverse, its square and its square root:

```
>> B = inv(A)
```

B =

```
  0.0711 - 0.2874i   0.5810 - 0.0806i   0.5407 + 0.8963i
 -0.0822 + 0.3322i  -0.3036 + 0.0932i  -0.6249 - 1.0359i
  0.2351 - 0.1418i   0.0659 - 0.0398i   0.2668 + 0.4423i
```

```
>> C = A^2
```

C =

```
  10.425 +      5i  72.422 +     10i  12.524 +      5i
  75.84 + 0.84147i  544.92 + 1.6829i  36.022 + 0.84147i
    -1  + 8.2832i      -2 + 51.281i       0 + 8.6829i
```

```
>> A ^ (1/2)
```

ans =

```
  0.7181 + 0.3784i  0.6691 - 0.6583i   2.0360 - 1.1395i
  1.2547 - 0.3193i  1.6690 + 0.3804i  -0.5550 + 0.8311i
 -0.1046 + 0.1852i  0.1152 + 0.5870i   1.2790 + 0.2869i
```

Now we check that the product of the matrix *A* with its inverse is the identity matrix of order 3:

```
>> A*B
```

ans =

```
  1.0000 + 0.0000i 0.0000 + 0.0000i 0.0000 + 0.0000i
  0.0000 + 0.0000i 1.0000 + 0.0000i 0.0000 + 0.0000i
  0.0000 + 0.0000i 0.0000 + 0.0000i 1.0000 + 0.0000i
```

Now we find the exponential of *A* with bases 2 and - 2:

```
>> 2^A
```

ans =

```
  1.0e+07 *
```

```
   0.0218 + 0.0057i    0.1569 + 0.0384i    0.0106 + 0.0031i
   0.1673 + 0.0176i    1.2036 + 0.1080i    0.0816 + 0.0110i
  -0.0024 + 0.0157i   -0.0156 + 0.1131i   -0.0014 + 0.0076i
```

```
>> (-2)^A
```

ans =

```
1.0e+06 *
```

```
   0.0585 - 0.1313i    0.4059 - 0.9492i    0.0305 - 0.0634i
   0.2852 - 1.0365i    1.9345 - 7.4766i    0.1545 - 0.5029i
   0.0965 + 0.0316i    0.6969 + 0.2161i    0.0468 + 0.0168i
```

So far, we have always worked with numeric matrices. To work with **symbolic matrices**, we simply define the variables to be symbolic using the command *syms*.

```
>>   syms t
>>   A=sym([sin(t),cos(t);tan(t),exp(t)])
```

A =

```
[sin (t), cos (t)]
[tan (t), exp (t)]
```

```
>> b = inv (A)
```

b =

```
[-exp (t) / (-sin (t) * exp (t) + cos (t) * tan (t)), cos (t) / (-sin (t) * exp (t) + cos (t)
* tan (t))]
```

```
[tan (t) / (-sin (t) * exp (t) + cos (t) * tan (t)), - sin (t) / (-sin (t) * exp (t) + cos
(t) * tan (t))]
```

1.6 Character Variables

MATLAB is a powerful numerical calculation program, but it is also a versatile character variable (i.e. text) manipulator. A character variable (or chain) is simply a string of characters contained within single quotes that MATLAB interprets as a vector form. For example:

>> c = 'string'

c =

character string

We have thus defined the character variable *c*. Among the MATLAB commands that handle character variables we have the following:

abs ('character_string')	*Returns the array of ASCII characters equivalent to each character in the string.*
setstr (numeric_vector)	*Returns the string of ASCII characters that are equivalent to the elements of the vector.*
str2mat (t1,t2,t3,...)	*Returns the matrix whose rows are the strings t1, t2, t3,..., respectively.*
str2num ('string')	*Converts the string to its exact numeric value used by MATLAB.*
num2str (number)	*Returns the exact number in its equivalent string with fixed precision.*
int2str (integer)	*Converts the integer to a string.*
sprintf ('format', a)	*Converts a numeric array into a string in the specified format.*
sscanf ('string', 'format')	*Converts a string to a numeric value in the specified format.*
dec2hex (integer)	*Converts a decimal integer into its equivalent string in hexadecimal.*
hex2dec ('string_hex')	*Converts a hexadecimal string into its integer equivalent.*
hex2num ('string_hex')	*Converts a hexadecimal string into the equivalent IEEE floating point number.*
lower ('string')	*Converts a string to lowercase.*
upper ('string')	*Converts a string to uppercase.*
strcmp (s1, s2)	*Compares the strings s1 and s2 and returns 1 if they are equal and 0 otherwise.*
strcmp (s1, s2, n)	*Compares the strings s1 and s2 and returns 1 if their first n characters are equal and 0 otherwise.*
strrep (c, 'exp1', 'exp2')	*Replaces exp1 by exp2 in the chain c.*
findstr (c, 'exp')	*Finds where exp is in the chain c.*
isstr (expression)	*Returns 1 if the expression is a string and 0 otherwise.*
ischar (expression)	*Returns 1 if the expression is a string and 0 otherwise.*
strjust (string)	*Right justifies the string.*
blanks (n)	*Generates a string of n spaces.*
deblank (string)	*Removes blank spaces from the right of the string.*
eval (expression)	*Executes the expression, even if it is a string.*
disp ('string')	*Displays the string (or array) as written, and continues the MATLAB process.*
input ('string')	*Displays the string on the screen and waits for a key press to continue.*

Here are some examples:

```
>> eval('4 * atan (1)')
```

ans =

3.1416

This shows how MATLAB numerically evaluates the contents of a string (according to the program's standard interpretation of the syntax).

```
>> hex2dec('3ffe56e')
```

ans =

67102062

MATLAB has converted a hexadecimal string to a decimal string.

```
>> dec2hex(1345679001)
```

ans =

50356E99

The program has converted a decimal string to a hexadecimal string.

```
>> sprintf('%f',[1+sqrt(5)/2,pi])
```

ans =

2.118034 3.141593

The exact numerical components of a vector have been converted to a string (to default precision).

```
>> sscanf('121.00012', '%f')
```

ans =

121.0001

A numeric string has been passed to exact numerical format (with default precision). Later we will see which alternative formats are possible.

```
>> num2str(pi)
```

ans =

3.142

The exact number π has been approximated to default precision and converted to a string.

>> str2num('15/14')

ans =

    1.0714

A string representing a rational number has been approximated to default precision and converted to a string.

>> setstr(32:126)

ans =

*!"#$% &' () * +, -. / 0123456789:; < = >? @ABCDEFGHIJKLMNOPQRSTUVWXYZ [\] ^*
_'abcdefghijklmnopqrstuvwxyz {|}~

The ASCII characters associated with whole numbers between 32 and 126 have been generated.

>> abs('{]}><#¡¿?º ª')

ans =

  123 93 125 62 60 35 161 191 63 186 170

The integers corresponding to the given ASCII characters have been generated.

>> lower('ABCDefgHIJ')

ans =

abcdefghij

The given string has been converted to lowercase text.

>> upper('abcd eFGHi jKlMn')

ans =

ABCD EFGHI JKLMN

The given string has been converted to uppercase text.

>> str2mat(' The world ',' The country ',' Daily 16 ', ' ABC ')

ans =

The world
The country
Daily 16
ABC

The chains given as arguments of the command *str2mat* have been converted into rows of an array.

>> disp('This text will appear on the screen')

This text will appear on the screen

The argument of the command *disp* is displayed on screen.

>> c = 'this is a good example';
>> strrep(c, 'good', 'bad')

ans =

this is a bad example

The string *good* has been replaced by the string *bad* in the string c.

>> findstr(c, 'is')

ans =

   3 6

The positions of the first character of the string *is* in *c* are given.

1.7 Operators

MATLAB features arithmetic, logical, relational, conditional and structural operators.

1.7.1 Arithmetic Operators

There are two types of arithmetic operators in MATLAB: matrix arithmetic operators, which are governed by the rules of linear algebra, and arithmetic operators on vectors, which are performed elementwise. The operators involved are presented in the following table. We have already seen these operations earlier.

Operator	Role played
+	*Sum of scalars, vectors, or matrices*
-	*Subtraction of scalars, vectors, or matrices*
*	*Product of scalars or arrays*
.*	*Product of scalars or vectors*
\	$A \backslash B = inv\ (A) * B$, *where A and B are matrices*
.\	$A.\backslash B = [B(i,j)/A\ (i,j)]$, *where A and B are vectors* $[dim\ (A) = dim\ (B)]$
/	*Quotient, or* $B/A = B * inv\ (A)$, *where A and B are matrices*
./	$A./B = [A(i,j)/B\ (i,j)]$, *where A and B are vectors* $[dim\ (A) = dim\ (B)]$
^	*Power of a scalar or matrix* (M^p)
.^	*Power of vectors* $(A.\wedge B = [A(i,j)^{B(i,j)}]$, *for vectors A and B)*

EXERCISE 1-9

Where X = [1 2 3] and Y = [4 5 6], calculate X + Y, X-Y, X * Y, X'* Y, X * Y', X.*Y, X.' * Y, X.*Y', 2 * X, 2.*X, X/Y, Y\X, X. / Y, Y\X, 2/X, 2. / X, 2\Y, 2. \Y, X ^ Y, X. ^ Y, X ^ 2, X^ 2, 2 ^ X and 2. ^ X.

```
>> X = [1,2,3]; Y = [4,5,6]; a = X + Y, b = X-Y, c = X * Y, d = 2. * X, e = 2/X,
f = 2. \Y, g = X. / Y, h =. \X, i = x ^ 2, j = 2. ^ X, k = x. ^ Y
```

a =

     5 7 9

b =

    -3 -3 -3

c =

     4 10 18

d =

     2   4   6

e =

    2.0000 1.0000 0.6667

f =

    2.0000 2.5000 3,0000

g =

    0.2500 0.4000 0.5000

h =

    0.2500 0.4000 0.5000

i =

     1 4 9

j =

   2 4 8

k =

   1 32 729

The above operations are all valid since in all cases the variable operands are of the same dimension, so the operations are successfully carried out element by element. For the sum and the difference there is no distinction between vectors and matrices, as the operations are identical in both cases.

>> X = [1,2,3]; Y = [4,5,6]; l = X'* Y, m = X * Y ', n = 2 * X, o = X / Y, p = Y\X

l =

   4   5   6
   8   10   12
  12   15   18

m =

   32

n =

   2 4 6

o =

   0.4156

p =

       0   0   0
       0   0   0
   0.1667   0.3333   0.5000

All of the above matrix operations are well defined since the dimensions of the operands are compatible in every case. We must not forget that a vector is a particular case of matrix, but to operate with it in matrix form (not element by element), it is necessary to respect the rules of dimensionality for matrix operations. For example, the vector operations *X. ' * Y* and *X.*Y'* make no sense, since they involve vectors of different dimensions. Similarly, the matrix operations *X * Y, 2/X, 2\Y, X ^ 2, 2 ^ X* and *X ^ Y* make no sense, again because of a conflict of dimensions in the arrays.

1.7.2 Relational Operators

MATLAB also provides relational operators. Relational operators perform element by element comparisons between two matrices and return an array of the same size whose elements are one if the corresponding relationship is true, or zero if the corresponding relation is false. The relational operators can also compare scalars with vectors or matrices, in which case the scalar is compared to all the elements of the array. Below is a table of these operators.

<	**Less than (for complex numbers this applies only to the real parts)**
< =	**Less than or equal (only applies to real parts of complex numbers)**
>	**Greater than (only applies to real parts of complex numbers)**
> =	**Greater than or equal (only applies to real parts of complex numbers)**
x == y	**Equality (also applies to complex numbers)**
x ~ = y	**Inequality (also applies to complex numbers)**

Here are some examples:

>> **X = 5 * ones (3,3); X > = [1 2 3; 4 5 6; 7 8 9]**

ans =

```
    1  1  1
    1  1  0
    0  0  0
```

The elements of the array X which are greater than or equal to the corresponding element of the matrix *[1 2 3; 4 5 6; 7 8 9]* are given the value 1 in the response matrix. The rest of the elements are assigned the value 0 (the result of the operation would have been the same if we had compared the scalar 5 to the matrix *[1 2 3; 4 5 6; 7 8 9]* using the expression $X = 5; X > = [1 2 3; 4 5 6; 7 8 9]$).

Next we see another example that combines an arithmetic operation with a relational operation:

>> **A = 1:9, B = 9-A, Y = A > 4, Z = B-(A>2)**

A =

```
    1    2    3    4    5    6    7    8    9
```

B =

```
    8    7    6    5    4    3    2    1    0
```

Y =

```
    0    0    0    0    1    1    1    1    1
```

Z =

```
    8    7    5    4    3    2    1    0   -1
```

The values of Y equal to 1 correspond to elements of A larger than 4. The Z values result from subtracting 1 from the corresponding elements of B if the corresponding element of A is greater than 2, or 0 if the corresponding element of A is less than or equal to 2.

1.7.3 Logical Operators

MATLAB provides symbols to denote logical operators. The logical operators shown in the following table offer a way to combine or negate relational expressions.

~ A	*Logical negation (NOT) or the complement of A.*
A & B	*Logical conjunction (AND) or the intersection of A and B.*
A | B	*Logical disjunction (OR) or the union of A and B.*
XOR (A, B)	*Exclusive OR (XOR) or the symmetric difference of A and B (takes the value 1 if A or B, but not both, are 1).*

Here are some examples:

```
>> A = 1:9; P = (A>2) & (A<6)
```

P =

```
    0    0    1    1    1    0    0    0    0
```

Returns 1 when A is greater than 2 and less than 6, and returns 0 otherwise.

```
>> A = [1 1 2 2 3 4 5 6 7 8 9],P = (A>=1)&(A<6),xor(A,P)
```

A =

```
    1    1    2    2    3    4    5    6    7    8    9
```

P =

```
    1    1    1    1    1    1    1    0    0    0    0
```

ans =

```
    0    0    0    0    0    0    0    1    1    1    1
```

Returns 1 when A or P, but not both, have the value 1.

1.8 Logic Functions

MATLAB implements logical functions whose output can take the value true (1) or false (0). The following table shows the most important logical functions.

exist(A)	*Checks if the variable or function exists (returns 0 if A does not exist and a number between 1 and 5, depending on the type, if it does exist).*
any(V)	*Returns 0 if all elements of the vector V are null and returns 1 if some element of V is non-zero.*
any(A)	*Returns 0 for each column of the matrix A with all null elements and returns 1 for each column of the matrix A which has non-null elements.*
all(V)	*Returns 1 if all the elements of the vector V are non-null and returns 0 if some element of V is null.*
all(A)	*Returns 1 for each column of the matrix A with all non-null elements and returns 0 for each column of the matrix A with at least one null element.*
find (V)	*Returns the places (or indices) occupied by the non-null elements of the vector V.*
isnan (V)	*Returns 1 for the elements of V that are indeterminate and returns 0 for those that are not.*
isinf (V)	*Returns 1 for the elements of V that are infinite and returns 0 for those that are not.*
isfinite (V)	*Returns 1 for the elements of V that are finite and returns 0 for those that are not.*
isempty (A)	*Returns 1 if A is an empty array and returns 0 otherwise (an empty array is an array such that one of its dimensions is 0).*
issparse (A)	*Returns 1 if A is a sparse matrix and returns 0 otherwise.*
isreal (V)	*Returns 1 if all the elements of V are real and 0 otherwise.*
isprime (V)	*Returns 1 for all elements of V that are prime and returns 0 for all elements of V that are not prime.*
islogical (V)	*Returns 1 if V is a logical vector and 0 otherwise.*
isnumeric (V)	*Returns 1 if V is a numeric vector and 0 otherwise.*
ishold	*Returns 1 if the properties of the current graph are retained for the next graph and only new elements will be added and 0 otherwise.*
isieee	*Returns 1 if the computer is capable of IEEE standard operations.*
isstr (S)	*Returns 1 if S is a string and 0 otherwise.*
ischart (S)	*Returns 1 if S is a string and 0 otherwise.*
isglobal (A)	*Returns 1 if A is a global variable and 0 otherwise.*
isletter (S)	*Returns 1 if S is a letter of the alphabet and 0 otherwise.*
isequal (A, B)	*Returns 1 if the matrices or vectors A and B are equal, and 0 otherwise.*
ismember (V, W)	*Returns 1 for every element of V which is in W and 0 for every element V that is not in W.*

Here are some examples:

```
>> isinf([pi NaN Inf - Inf])
```

ans =

    0   0   1   1

```
>> any([pi NaN Inf -Inf])
```

ans =

    1

```
>> ismember([1,2,3,5],[8,12,1,3,56,5])
```

ans =

    1   0   1   1

```
>> A = [2,0,1]; B = [4,0,2];
>> isequal(2*A,B)
```

ans =

    1

```
>> V = [-10,5,3,12,0];
>> isprime(V)
```

ans =

    0   1   1   0   0

```
>> isnumeric(V)
```

ans =

    1

```
>> all(V)
```

ans =

    0

```
>> any(V)
```

ans =

    1

```
>> C = [0 2 3; 0 1 2;0 4 6],D = [0 0 0 0;4 3 1 2;6 0 0 4]
>> any(C),all(C),any(D),all(D)
```

ans =

    0 1 1

ans =

    0 1 1

ans =

    1 1 1 1

ans =

    0 0 0 0

1.9 Elementary Functions that Support Complex Matrix Arguments

- **Trigonometric**

sin (z)	*Sine function*
sinh (z)	*Hyperbolic sine function*
asin (z)	*Arcsine function*
asinh (z)	*Hyperbolic arcsine function*
cos (z)	*Cosine function*
cosh (z)	*Hyperbolic cosine function*
acos (z)	*Arccosine function*
acosh (z)	*Hyperbolic arccosine function*
tan(z)	*Tangent function*
tanh (z)	*Hyperbolic tangent function*
atan (z)	*Arctangent function*
atan2 (z)	*Fourth quadrant arctangent function*
atanh (z)	*Hyperbolic arctangent function*
sec (z)	*Secant function*
sech (z)	*Hyperbolic secant function*
asec (z)	*Arccosecant function*
asech (z)	*Hyperbolic arccosecant function*
csc (z)	*Cosecant function*

(continued)

csch (z)	*Hyperbolic cosecant function*
acsc (z)	*Arccosecant function*
acsch (z)	*Hyperbolic arccosecant function*
cot (z)	*Cotangent function*
coth (z)	*Hyperbolic cotangent function*
acot (z)	*Arccotangent function*
acoth (z)	*Hyperbolic arccotangent function*

- **Exponential**

exp (z)	*Base e exponential function*
log (z)	*Natural logarithm function (base e)*
log10 (z)	*Base 10 logarithm function*
sqrt (z)	*Square root function*

- **Complex**

abs (z)	*Modulus or absolute value*
angle (z)	*Argument*
conj (z)	*Complex conjugate*
imag (z)	*Imaginary part*
real (z)	*Real part*

- **Numerical**

fix (z)	*Removes the fractional part*
floor (z)	*Rounds to the nearest lower integer*
ceil (z)	*Rounds to the nearest greater integer*
round (z)	*Performs common rounding*
rem (z1, z2)	*Returns the remainder of the division of z1 by z2*
sign (z)	*The sign of z*

- **Matrix**

expm (Z)	*Matrix exponential function by default*
expm1 (Z)	*Matrix exponential function in M-file*
expm2 (Z)	*Matrix exponential function via Taylor series*
expm3 (Z)	*Matrix exponential function via eigenvalues*
logm (Z)	*Logarithmic matrix function*
sqrtm (Z)	*Matrix square root function*
funm(Z,'function')	*Applies the function to the array Z*

Here are some examples:

```
>> A = [1 2 3; 4 5 6;7 8 9]
```

A =

```
    1      2      3
    4      5      6
    7      8      9
```

```
>> sin(A)
```

ans =

```
   0.8415   0.9093   0.1411
  -0.7568  -0.9589  -0.2794
   0.6570   0.9894   0.4121
```

```
>> B = [1+i 2+i;3+i,4+i]
```

B =

```
   1.0000 + 1.0000i 2.0000 + 1.0000i
   3.0000 + 1.0000i 4.0000 + 1.0000i
```

```
>> sin(B)
```

ans =

```
   1.2985 + 0.6350i   1.4031 - 0.4891i
   0.2178 - 1.1634i  -1.1678 - 0.7682i
```

```
>> exp(A)
```

ans =

```
  1.0e + 003 *

   0.0027 0.0074 0.0201
   0.0546 0.1484 0.4034
   1.0966 2.9810 8.1031
```

>> exp(B)

ans =

```
    1.4687 + 2.2874i    3.9923 + 6.2177i
   10.8523 +16.9014i   29.4995 +45.9428i
```

>> log(B)

ans =

```
    0.3466 + 0.7854i    0.8047 + 0.4636i
    1.1513 + 0.3218i    1.4166 + 0.2450i
```

>> sqrt(B)

ans =

```
    1.0987 + 0.4551i    1.4553 + 0.3436i
    1.7553 + 0.2848i    2.0153 + 0.2481i
```

The exponential functions, square root and logarithm used above apply to the array elementwise and have nothing to do with the matrix exponential and logarithmic functions that are used below.

>> expm(B)

ans =

```
    1.0e+002 *

   -0.3071 + 0.4625i   -0.3583 + 0.6939i
   -0.3629 + 1.0431i   -0.3207 + 1.5102i
```

>> logm(A)

ans =

```
   -5.6588 + 2.7896i   12.5041 - 0.4325i   -5.6325 - 0.5129i
   12.8139 - 0.7970i  -23.3307 + 2.1623i   13.1237 - 1.1616i
   -5.0129 - 1.2421i   13.4334 - 1.5262i   -4.4196 + 1.3313i
```

>> abs(B)

ans =

```
    1.4142    2.2361
    3.1623    4.1231
```

```
>> imag(B)
```

ans =

```
    1     1
    1     1
```

```
>> fix(sin(B))
```

ans =

```
   1.0000           1.0000
   0 - 1.0000i     -1.0000
```

```
>> ceil(log(A))
```

ans =

```
    0     1     2
    2     2     2
    2     3     3
```

```
>> sign(B)
```

ans =

```
   0.7071 + 0.7071i   0.8944 + 0.4472i
   0.9487 + 0.3162i   0.9701 + 0.2425i
```

```
>> rem(A,3*ones(3))
```

ans =

```
    1     2     0
    1     2     0
    1     2     0
```

```
>> funm(B,'sinh')
```

ans =

```
   -15.8616 +23.2384i -17.6536 +34.7072i
   -17.7736 +52.1208i -16.2216 +75.4791i
```

The result of the last function is equivalent to *sinh(B)*, but the algorithm used is different.

1.10 Elementary Functions that Support Complex Vector Arguments

max (V)	*The maximum component of V. (max is calculated for complex vectors as the complex number with the largest complex modulus (magnitude), computed with max(abs(V)). Then it computes the largest phase angle with max(angle(x)), if necessary.)*
min (V)	*The minimum component of V. (min is calculated for complex vectors as the complex number with the smallest complex modulus (magnitude), computed with min(abs(A)). Then it computes the smallest phase angle with min(angle(x)), if necessary.)*
mean (V)	*Average of the components of V.*
median (V)	*Median of the components of V.*
std (V)	*Standard deviation of the components of V.*
sort (V)	*Sorts the components of V in ascending order. For complex entries the order is by absolute value and argument.*
sum (V)	*Returns the sum of the components of V.*
prod (V)	*Returns the product of the components of V, so, for example, n! = prod(1:n).*
cumsum (V)	*Gives the cumulative sums of the components of V.*
cumprod (V)	*Gives the cumulative products of the components of V.*
diff (V)	*Gives the vector of first differences of V (V_t - V_{t-1}).*
gradient (V)	*Gives the gradient of V.*
del2 (V)	*Gives the Laplacian of V (5-point discrete).*
fft (V)	*Gives the discrete Fourier transform of V.*
fft2 (V)	*Gives the two-dimensional discrete Fourier transform of V.*
ifft (V)	*Gives the inverse discrete Fourier transform of V.*
ifft2 (V)	*Gives the inverse two-dimensional discrete Fourier transform of V.*

These functions also support a complex matrix as an argument, in which case the result is a vector of column vectors whose components are the results of applying the function to each column of the matrix.

Here are some examples:

```
>> V = 1:5, W = [1-i 2i 2 + 3i]
```

V =

    1   2   3   4   5

W =

   1.0000 - 1.0000i   0 + 2.0000i   2.0000 + 3.0000i

>> diff(V)

ans =

   1   1   1   1

>> diff(W)

ans =

  -1.0000 + 3.0000i   2.0000 + 1.0000i

>> cumprod(V)

ans =

   1   2   6   24   120

>> cumsum(W)

ans =

   1.0000 - 1.0000i   1.0000 + 1.0000i   3.0000 + 4.0000i

>> mean(W)

ans =

   1.0000 + 1.3333i

>> std(V)

ans =

   1.5811

>> sort(W)

ans =

   1.0000 - 1.0000i   0 + 2.0000i   2.0000 + 3.0000i

>> sum(W)

ans =

   3.0000 + 4.0000i

>> **prod(V)**

ans =

   120

>> **gradient(W)**

ans =

  -1.0000 + 3.0000i   0.5000 + 2.0000i   2.0000 + 1.0000i

>> **del2(W)**

ans =

        0   1.5000 - 1.0000i   0

>> **fft(W)**

ans =

   3.0000 + 4.0000i   -0.8660 - 1.7679i   0.8660 - 5.2321i

>> **ifft(W)**

ans =

   1.0000 + 1.3333i   0.2887 - 1.7440i   -0.2887 - 0.5893i

>> **fft2(W)**

ans =

   3.0000 + 4.0000i   - 0.8660 - 1.7679i   0.8660 - 5.2321i

1.11 Vector Functions of Several Variables

Functions of one or several variables are defined via the command *maple* as follows:

> maple ('f: = x - > f (x)') or maple f: = x - > f (x) **defines the function** $f(x)$

> maple ('f:=(x,y,z...))(- > f(x,y,z...)') **defines the function** $f(x,y,z,..)$

> maple ('f:=(x,y,z...))(- > (f1 (x, y...), f2(x,y..),...)') **defines the vector function** $(f1(x,y,..), f2(x,y,..),...)$

To find the value of the function $(x, y, z) - > f(x,y,z...)$ at the point $(a, b, c,...)$ the expression *maple ('f(a,b,c,...)')* is used.

We find the value of the vector function $f:=(x,y,..)-> (f1(x,y,..), f2(x,y,..),...)$ at the point $(a, b,...)$ by using the expression **maple ('f(a,b,..)')**.

The function $f(x,y) = 2x + y$ is defined in the following way:

```
>> maple('f:=(x,y) - > 2 * x + y ');
```

$f\ (2,3)$ and $f(a,b)$ are calculated as follows:

```
>> maple('f(2,3)')
```

ans =

7

```
>> maple('f(a,b)')
```

ans =

2 * a + b

EXERCISE 1-10

Given the function h defined by: $h(x,y) = (\cos(x^2-y^2), \sin(x^2-y^2))$, calculate h (1,2), h(-Pi,Pi) and h (cos (a^2), cos (1 -a^2)).

As *h* is a vector function of two variables, we use the command *maple*:

```
>> maple ('h:=(x,y) - > (cos(x^2-y^2), sin(x^2-y^2))');
>> maple ('A = h (1, 2), B = h(-pi,pi), C = h (cos(a^2), cos(1-a^2))')
```

ans =

A = (cos (3),-sin(3)), B = (1, 0),
C = (cos (cos(a^2) ^ 2-cos(-1+a^2) ^ 2), sin(cos(a^2) ^ 2-cos(-1+a^2) ^ 2))

1.11.1 Functions of One Variable

Functions of one variable are a special case of functions of several variables, but they can also be defined in MATLAB via the command $f = $ *'function'*.

To find the value of the function *f* at a point, you use the command ***subs***, whose syntax is as follows:

> **subs(f, a) applies the function *f* at the point *a***

> **subs (f, a, b) assigns the value of the function at the point *a* to the variable *b***

Let's see how to define the function $f(x) = x \wedge 2$:

```
>> f = 'x ^ 2'
```

f =

x ^ 2

Now we calculate the values $f(4)$, $f(a+1)$ and $f(3x+x^2)$:

```
>> syms a x
>> A = subs(f,4),B = subs(f,a+1),C = subs(f,3*x+x^2)

A =

16

B =

(a+1) ^ 2

C =

(3 * x + x ^ 2) ^ 2
```

It should also be borne in mind that if we use the command *maple*, the special constants π, e, i, and ∞ are defined as *maple('Pi')*, *maple ('exp (1)')*, *maple('i')* and *maple('infinity')* respectively.

EXERCISE 1-11

Define the functions f $(x) = x^2$, $g(x) = x^{1/2}$ and $h(x) = x + \sin(x)$. Calculate f(2), g(4) and h(a-b^2).

```
>> f = 'x ^ 2'; g = 'x ^(1/2)'; h = 'x+sin (x)';

>> syms a b
>> a = subs(f,2),b = subs(g,4),c = subs(h,'a-b^2')

a =

4

b =

4^(1/2)

c =

a-b ^ 2 + sin(a-b^2)
```

We could also have done the following:

```
>> maple('f:=x->x^2: g:=x->sqrt(x):h:=x->x+sin(x)');
>> maple('f(2),g(4),h(a-b^2)')

ans =

4, 2, a-b ^ 2 + sin(a-b^2)
```

CHAPTER 2

■ ■ ■

Matrix Algebra

2.1 Vectors and Matrices

We have already seen how vectors and matrices are represented in MATLAB in the chapter dedicated to variables, however we shall recall here the notation.

Consider the matrix

$$A = (A_{ij}) = \begin{pmatrix} a_{11} & a_{12} & a_{13} & \cdots & a_{1n} \\ a_{21} & a_{22} & a_{23} & \cdots & a_{2n} \\ a_{31} & a_{32} & a_{33} & \cdots & a_{3n} \\ \cdots & \cdots & \cdots & \cdots & \cdots \\ a_{m1} & a_{m2} & a_{m3} & \cdots & a_{mn} \end{pmatrix},$$

$$i = 1,2,3,\ldots,m \quad j = 1,2,3,\ldots,n.$$

You can enter this in MATLAB in the following ways:

A=[a11,a12,...,a1n ; a21,a22,...,a2n ; ... ; am1,am2,...,amn]

A=[a11 a12 ... a1n ; a21 a22 ... a2n ; ... ; am1 am2 ... amn]

A=maple('array([[a11,..,a1n],[a21,..,a2n],..,[am1,..,amn]])')

A=maple('matrix(m,n,[a11,..,a1n,a21,..,a2n,..,am1,..,amn])')

A=maple('matrix([[a11,..,a1n],[a21,..,a2n],..,[am1,..,amn]])')

On the other hand, a vector $V = (v1, v2, \ldots, vn)$ is introduced as a special case of a matrix with a single row (i.e. a matrix of dimension $1 \times n$) in the following form:

V = [v1, v2,..., vn]

V = [v1 v2... vn]

V = maple ('vector([v1, v2,..., vn])')

V = maple ('vector(n,[v1, v2,..., vn])')

V=maple('array([v1, v2, ..., vn])')

2.2 Operations with Numeric Matrices

MATLAB supports the most common matrix algebra operations (sum, difference, product, scalar product), provided the dimensionality conditions hold.

The common MATLAB matrix commands are summarized below.

A + B sum of matrices *A* and *B*

A − B difference of the matrices *A* and *B* (*A* minus *B*)

c * M product of the scalar *c* and the matrix *M*

A * B product of the matrices *A* and *B*

A ^ p matrix *A* raised to the power of the scalar *p*

p ^ A scalar *p* raised to the power of the matrix *A*

expm1 (A) e^A calculated via Padé approximants

expm2 (A) e^A calculated via Taylor series

expm3 (A) e^A calculated via eigenvalues and eigenvectors

logm(A) (Napierian logarithm of the matrix A)

sqrtm (A) square root of the matrix *A*

funm (A, 'function') applies the function to the matrix *A*

transpose (A) or *A*' transpose of the matrix *A*

inv (A) inverse of the square matrix *A* (A^{-1})

det (A) determinant of the square matrix *A*

rank (A) range of the matrix *A*

trace (A) sum of the elements of the diagonal of *A*

svd (A) gives the vector V of singular values of *A*. The singular values of *A* are the square roots of the eigenvalues of the symmetric matrix *A*' *A*.

[U, S, V] = svd (A) gives the diagonal matrix *S* of singular values of *A* (ordered from largest to smallest), and the matrices *U* and *V* such that A= *U* * *S* * *V*'.

cond (A) gives the condition number of the matrix *A* (the ratio between the largest and the smallest singular values of *A*)

rcond (A) the reciprocal condition number of the matrix *A*

norm (A) the standard or 2-norm of *A* (the largest singular value of *A*)

norm(A,1) the 1-norm of A (the maximum column magnitude, where the column magnitude of a column is the sum of the absolute values of its elements)

norm(A,inf) the infinity norm of *A* (the maximum row magnitude, where the row magnitude of a row is the sum of the absolute values of its elements)

norm(A,'fro') the Frobenius norm of *A*, defined by *sqrt (sum (diag(A'A)))*

Z = null (A) gives an orthonormal basis for the null space of A obtained from the singular value decomposition, i.e. AZ has negligible elements, size(Z,2) is the nullity of A, and Z′Z = I.

Q = orth (A) *Returns an orthonormal basis for the range of A, Q′Q=I. The columns of Q are vectors which span the range of A. The number of columns in Q is equal to the rank of A.*

subspace (A, B) *finds the angle between two subspaces specified by the columns of A and B. If A and B are column vectors of unit length, this is the same as acos(abs(A′*B)).*

rref (A) *produces the reduced row echelon form of A using Gauss-Jordan elimination with partial pivoting. The number of non-zero rows of rref (A) is the rank of A.*

Here are some examples:

We consider the matrix $M = [1/3,1/4,1/5;1/4,1/5,1/6; 1/5,1/6,1/7]$, and find its transpose, its inverse, its determinant, its range, its trace, its singular values, its condition number, its norm, M^3, e^M, $log (M)$ and $sqrt (M)$:

```
>> M = [1/3,1/4,1/5; 1/4,1/5,1/6; 1/5,1/6,1/7]
```

M =

```
    0.3333 0.2500 0.2000
    0.2500 0.2000 0.1667
    0.2000 0.1667 0.1429
```

```
>> transpose = M'
```

transpose =

```
    0.3333 0.2500 0.2000
    0.2500 0.2000 0.1667
    0.2000 0.1667 0.1429
```

```
>> inverse = inv (M)
```

inverse =

```
  1. 0e + 003 *

    0.3000   -0.9000   0.6300
   -0.9000    2.8800  -2.1000
    0.6300   -2.1000   1.5750
```

To verify that the inverse has been calculated, we multiply it by *M* and check that the result is the identity matrix of order 3:

```
>> M * inv (M)
```

ans =

```
    1.0000 0.0000 0.0000
    0.0000 1.0000 0.0000
    0.0000 0.0000 1.0000
```

```
>> determinant = det (M)
```

determinant =

   2. 6455e-006

```
>> rank=rank(M)
```

rank =

     3

```
>> trace=trace(M)
```

trace =

   0.6762

```
>> vsingular = svd (M)
```

vsingular =

   0.6571
   0.0189
   0.0002

```
>> condition =cond(M)
```

condition =

  3. 0886e + 003

For the calculation of the norm, we find the standard norm, the 1-norm, the infinity norm and the Frobenius norm:

```
>> norm(M)
```

ans =

   0.6571

```
>> norm(M,1)
```

ans =

   0.7833

```
>> norm(M,inf)
```

ans =

   0.7833

```
>> norm(M,'fro')
```

ans =

    0.6573

```
>> M^3
```

ans =

    0.1403   0.1096   0.0901
    0.1096   0.0856   0.0704
    0.0901   0.0704   0.0578

```
>> logm(M)
```

ans =

   -2.4766   2.2200   0.5021
    2.2200   -5.6421   2.8954
    0.5021   2.8954   -4.7240

```
>> sqrtm(M)
```

ans =

    0.4631 0.2832 0.1966
    0.2832 0.2654 0.2221
    0.1966 0.2221 0.2342

The variants using eigenvalues, Padé approximants and Taylor series will be used to calculate e^M:

```
>> expm(M)
```

ans =

    1.4679   0.3550   0.2863
    0.3550   1.2821   0.2342
    0.2863   0.2342   1.1984

```
>> expm1(M)
```

ans =

    1.4679   0.3550   0.2863
    0.3550   1.2821   0.2342
    0.2863   0.2342   1.1984

```
>> expm2(M)
```

ans =

```
    1.4679    0.3550    0.2863
    0.3550    1.2821    0.2342
    0.2863    0.2342    1.1984
```

```
>> expm3(M)
```

As we see, the exponential matrix coincides using all methods.

EXERCISE 2-1

Given the three matrices

$$A = \begin{bmatrix} 1 & 1 & 0 \\ 0 & 1 & 1 \\ 0 & 0 & 1 \end{bmatrix} \quad B = \begin{bmatrix} i & 1-i & 2+i \\ 0 & -1 & 3-i \\ 0 & 0 & -i \end{bmatrix} \quad C = \begin{bmatrix} 1 & 1 & 1 \\ 0 & sqrt(2)i & -sqrt(2)i \\ 1 & -1 & -1 \end{bmatrix}$$

calculate AB - BA, $A^2 + B^2 + C^2$, ABC, sqrt (A) + sqrt (B) + sqrt (C), e^A ($e^B + e^C$) and find the range, inverse, trace, determinant, condition number and singular values of A, B and C.

```
>> A=[1 1 0;0 1 1;0 0 1]; B=[i 1-i 2+i;0 -1 3-i;0 0 -i];
   C=[1 1 1; 0 sqrt(2)*i -sqrt(2)*i;1 -1 -1];
```

```
>> M1=A*B-B*A
```

M1 =

```
     0          -1.0000 - 1.0000i    2.0000
     0                  0            1.0000 - 1.0000i
     0                  0                  0
```

```
>> M2=A^2+B^2+C^2
```

M2 =

```
    2.0000          2.0000 + 3.4142i    3.0000 - 5.4142i
        0 - 1.4142i    0.0000 + 1.4142i    0.0000 - 0.5858i
        0              2.0000 - 1.4142i    2.0000 + 1.4142i
```

```
>> M3=A*B*C
```

M3 =

```
  5.0000 + 1.0000i  -3.5858 + 1.0000i  -6.4142 + 1.0000i
  3.0000 - 2.0000i  -3.0000 + 0.5858i  -3.0000 + 3.4142i
       0 - 1.0000i       0 + 1.0000i       0 + 1.0000i
```

```
>> M4=sqrtm(A)+sqrtm(B)-sqrtm(C)
```

M4 =

```
  0.6356 + 0.8361i  -0.3250 - 0.8204i   3.0734 + 1.2896i
  0.1582 - 0.1521i   0.0896 + 0.5702i   3.3029 - 1.8025i
 -0.3740 - 0.2654i   0.7472 + 0.3370i   1.2255 + 0.1048i
```

```
>> M5=expm(A)*(expm(B)+expm(C))
```

M5 =

```
 14.1906 - 0.0822i   5.4400 + 4.2724i  17.9169 - 9.5842i
  4.5854 - 1.4972i   0.6830 + 2.1575i   8.5597 - 7.6573i
  3.5528 + 0.3560i   0.1008 - 0.7488i   3.2433 - 1.8406i
```

```
>> ranks=[rank(A) rank(B) rank(C)]
```

ranks =

```
    3    3    3
```

```
>> vsingular=[svd(A),svd(B),svd(C)]
```

vsingular =

```
  1.8019    4.2130    2.0000
  1.2470    1.4917    2.0000
  0.4450    0.1591    1.4142
```

```
>> traces=[trace(A) trace(B) trace(C)]
```

traces =

```
  3.0000            -1.0000                0 + 1.4142i
```

```
>> inv(A)
```

ans =

```
    1   -1    1
    0    1   -1
    0    0    1
```

>> **inv(B)**

ans =

```
      0 - 1.0000i  -1.0000 - 1.0000i  -4.0000 + 3.0000i
      0                  -1.0000       1.0000 + 3.0000i
      0                        0            0 + 1.0000i
```

>> **inv(C)**

ans =

```
   0.5000                 0           0.5000
   0.2500        0 - 0.3536i         -0.2500
   0.2500        0 + 0.3536i         -0.2500
```

>> **determinants = [det(A) det (B) det (C)]**

determinants =

```
   1.0000 - 1.0000 0 - 5. 6569i
```

>> **conditions = [cond(A) cond (B) cond(C)]**

conditions =

```
   4.0489 26.4765 1,4142
```

EXERCISE 2-2

Consider the following matrix:

$$M = \begin{bmatrix} 1/3 & 1/4 & 1/5 \\ 1/4 & 1/5 & 1/6 \\ 1/5 & 1/6 & 1/7 \end{bmatrix}$$

Find its transpose, its inverse, its determinant, its range, its trace, its singular values, its condition number, its norm and M^3, regarded as a symbolic matrix.

>> **M = sym ('[1/3,1/4,1/5; 1/4,1/5,1/6; 1/5,1/6,1/7]')**

M =

```
[1/3,1/4,1/5]
[1/4,1/5,1/6]
[1/5,1/6,1/7]
```

>> transpose = transpose (M)

transpose =

[1/3, 1/4, 1/5]
[1/4, 1/5, 1/6]
[1/5, 1/6, 1/7]

>> inverse = inv (M)

inverse =

[300,   -900,   630]
[-900,   2880, -2100]
[630, -2100,   1575]

>> determinant=det (M)

determinant =

1/378000

>> rank=rank(M)

rank =

3

>> trace=trace(M)

trace =

71/105

>> numeric(svd (M))

ans =

   0.6571
   0.0002 - 0.0000i
   0.0189 + 0.0000i

>> norm = maple ('norm([[1/3,1/4,1/5],[1/4,1/5,1/6],[1/5,1/6,1/7]])')

norm =

47/60

```
>> sympow(M,3)
```

ans =

```
[10603/75600,      1227/11200,   26477/294000]
[1227/11200,     10783/126000,  74461/1058400]
[26477/294000,   74461/1058400,   8927/154350]
```

Now we find the norms and condition number of M as a numeric matrix:

```
>> [norm(numeric(M)),norm(numeric(M),1),cond(numeric(M),inf),
cond(numeric(M),'fro'),normest(numeric(M))]
```

ans =

   1.0e+003 *

0.0008   4.6060   3.0900   0.0007   0.8

```
>> [cond(numeric(M),1),cond(numeric(M),2),cond(numeric(M),'fro'),
condest(numeric(M))]
```

ans =

   1.0e+003 *

     4.6060   3.0886   3.0900   4.6060

EXERCISE 2-3

Define a square matrix A of dimension 5 whose elements are given by A(i,j) = $i^3 - j^2$. Extract the submatrix of A formed by rows 2 to 4 and columns 3 to 4. Delete rows 2 to 4 of the matrix A, as well as column 5. Exchange the first and last rows of the matrix A. Exchange the first and last columns of the matrix A. Insert a column of 1s to the right of the matrix A. Insert a column of 1s to the left of the matrix A. Insert two rows of 1s at the top of the matrix A. Perform the same operation at the bottom.

First, we generate the matrix *A* as follows:

```
>> A=sym(maple('matrix(5,5,(i,j)-> i^3-j^2)'))
```

A =

```
[   0,   -3,   -8,  -15,  -24]
[   7,    4,   -1,   -8,  -17]
[  26,   23,   18,   11,    2]
[  63,   60,   55,   48,   39]
[ 124,  121,  116,  109,  100]
```

```
>> maple('A:=matrix(5,5,(i,j)-> i^3-j^2)');
>> sym(maple('submatrix(A,2..4,3..4)'))
```

ans =

```
[ -1,  -8]
[ 18,  11]
[ 55,  48]
```

```
>> sym(maple('delrows(A,2..4)'))
```

ans =

```
[   0,   -3,   -8,  -15,  -24]
[ 124,  121,  116,  109,  100]
```

```
>> sym(maple('delcols(A,5..5)'))
```

ans =

```
[   0,   -3,   -8,  -15]
[   7,    4,   -1,   -8]
[  26,   23,   18,   11]
[  63,   60,   55,   48]
[ 124,  121,  116,  109]
```

```
>> pretty(sym(maple('swapcol(A,1,5),swaprow(A,1,5)')))
```

```
    [-24     -3      -8     -15      0]  [124    121     116     109     100]
    [                                 ]  [                                  ]
    [-17      4      -1      -8      7]  [  7      4      -1      -8     -17]
    [                                 ]  [                                  ]
    [  2     23      18      11     26],  [ 26     23      18      11      2]
    [                                 ]  [                                  ]
    [ 39     60      55      48     63]  [ 63     60      55      48      39]
    [                                 ]  [                                  ]
    [100    121     116     109    124]  [  0     -3      -8     -15     -24]
```

```
>> maple('B:=array([1,1,1,1,1])');
>> pretty(sym(maple('augment(A,B),augment(B,A)')));
```

```
    [  0     -3      -8     -15     -24    1]  [1      0      -3      -8     -15    -24]
    [                                      ]  [                                      ]
    [  7      4      -1      -8     -17    1]  [1      7       4      -1      -8    -17]
    [                                      ]  [                                      ]
    [ 26     23      18      11      2    1],  [1     26      23      18      11      2]
    [                                      ]  [                                      ]
    [ 63     60      55      48     39    1]  [1     63      60      55      48     39]
    [                                      ]  [                                      ]
    [124    121     116     109    100    1]  [1    124     121     116     109    100]
```

```
>> maple('C:=array([[1,1,1,1,1],[1,1,1,1,1]])');
>> pretty(sym(maple('stack(C,A),stack(A,C)')));
```

```
[   1      1      1      1      1]  [   0     -3     -8    -15    -24]
[                                ]  [                                ]
[   1      1      1      1      1]  [   7      4     -1     -8    -17]
[                                ]  [                                ]
[   0     -3     -8    -15    -24]  [  26     23     18     11      2]
[                                ]  [                                ]
[   7      4     -1     -8    -17], [  63     60     55     48     39]
[                                ]  [                                ]
[  26     23     18     11      2]  [ 124    121    116    109    100]
[                                ]  [                                ]
[  63     60     55     48     39]  [   1      1      1      1      1]
[                                ]  [                                ]
[ 124    121    116    109    100]  [   1      1      1      1      1]
```

2.3 Eigenvalues and Eigenvectors

2.3.1 Numeric Matrices

MATLAB enables commands that allow you to work with eigenvalues and eigenvectors of a square matrix. For *numeric matrices*, we have the following:

eig(A) Finds the eigenvalues of the square matrix A.

[V, D] = eig (A) Returns the diagonal matrix D of eigenvalues of A, and a matrix V whose columns are the corresponding eigenvectors, so that A * V = V * D.

eig(A,B) Returns a vector with the generalized eigenvalues of the square matrices A and B. The generalized eigenvalues of A and B are the roots of the polynomial in λ: det (λ * B - A).

[V, D] = eig (A, B) returns the diagonal matrix D of generalized eigenvalues of A and B and a matrix V whose columns are the corresponding eigenvectors, so that A * V = B * V * D.

[AA, BB, Q, Z, V] = qz (A, B)

Calculates the upper triangular matrices AA and BB and matrices Q and Z such that Q * A * Z = Q and AA * B * Z = BB, and gives the matrix V of generalized eigenvectors of A and B, so that A * V * diag (BB) = B * V * diag (AA).

[T, B] = balance (A) Returns a similarity transformation T such that B = T\A*T, and B has, as closely as possible, approximately equal row and column norms. The matrix B is called the balanced matrix of A.

balance(A) Computes the balanced matrix B of A. This is used to approximate the eigenvalues of A when they are difficult to estimate. We have eig (A) = eig (balance (A)).

[V, D] = cdf2rdf (V, D) If the eigensystem [V,D]= eig(X) has complex eigenvalues appearing in complex-conjugate pairs, cdf2rdf transforms the system so D is in real diagonal form, with 2×2 real blocks along the diagonal replacing the original complex pairs. The eigenvectors are transformed so that X = V*D/V continues to hold.

[U, T] = schur (A) Returns a matrix *T* and a unitary matrix *U* such that *A* = *U* * *T* * *U'* and *U'** *U* = *eye (U)*. If *A* is complex, *T* is an upper triangular matrix with the eigenvalues of *A* on its diagonal. If *A* is real, *T* has the eigenvalues of *A* on its diagonal, and the corresponding complex eigenvalues correspond to the 2 × 2 diagonal blocks of *T*.

Schur (A) Returns only the matrix *T* of the above decomposition.

[U, T] = rsf2csf (U, T) Converts the real Schur form to the complex form.

[H, P] = hess (A) Returns the unitary matrix *P* and Hessenberg matrix *H* such that *A* = *P* * *H* * *P'* and *P'** *P* = *eye (size (P))*.

hess (A) Returns the Hessenberg matrix of *A*.

poly (A) Returns the characteristic polynomial of the matrix *A*.

poly (V) Returns a vector whose components are the coefficients of the polynomial whose roots are the elements of the vector *V*.

vander (C) Returns the Vandermonde matrix *A* such that its j-th column is *A(:,j)* = *C* ^ *(n-j)*.

EXERCISE 2-4

Consider the matrix:

$$M = \begin{bmatrix} 1 & -1 & 3 \\ -1 & i & -1-2i \\ i & 1 & i-2 \end{bmatrix}$$

Compute its eigenvalues and eigenvectors, the balanced matrix with its eigenvalues, and its characteristic polynomial.

```
>> A=[1,-1,3;-1,i,-1-2i;i,1,i-2];
>> [V,D] = eig(A)
```

V =

```
   0.9129            0.1826 + 0.5477i  -0.1826 + 0.3651i
  -0.2739 - 0.0913i  0.5477 - 0.1826i   0.3651 - 0.7303i
  -0.0913 + 0.2739i -0.1826 - 0.5477i   0.1826 - 0.3651i
```

D =

```
  1.0000 + 1.0000i  0                 0
  0                -2.0000 + 1.0000i  0
  0                 0                 0
```

We see that the eigenvalues of A are 1 + i, −2 + i and 0, and the eigenvectors are the columns of the matrix V. We now calculate the balanced matrix of A and verify that its eigenvalues coincide with those of A:

```
>> balance(A)
```

ans =

```
   1.0000          -1.0000           1.5000
  -1.0000           0 + 1.0000i     -0.5000 - 1.0000i
   0 + 2.0000i      2.0000          -2.0000 + 1.0000i
```

```
>> eig(balance(A))
```

ans =

```
 1.0000 + 1.0000i
-2.0000 + 1.0000i
 0
```

We now calculate the characteristic of polynomial of A:

```
>> p=poly(A)
```

p =

```
  1.0000    1.0000 - 2.0000i  -3.0000 - 1.0000i     0
```

```
>> vpa(poly2sym(p))
```

ans =

```
x^3+x^2-2.*i*x^2-3.*x-1.*i*x
```

Thus, the characteristic polynomial is $x^3 + x^2 - 2ix^2 - 3x - ix$.

2.3.2 Symbolic Matrices

EXERCISE 2-5

Consider the square matrix A of order 5 whose (i, j)th element is given by $1/(i+j-1/2)$. Compute the eigenvalues, eigenvectors, characteristic polynomial, minimum polynomial, characteristic matrix and singular values of A. Also find the vector of condition numbers of the eigenvalues and analyze whether A is positive definite, negative definite or positive or negative semidefinite.

MATLAB enables you to define this type of symbolic matrix in the general form:

```
>> A=sym(maple('matrix(5,5,(i,j)-> 1/(i+j-1/2))'))
```

A =

```
[ 2/3,   2/5,   2/7,   2/9, 2/11]
[ 2/5,   2/7,   2/9,  2/11, 2/13]
[ 2/7,   2/9,  2/11,  2/13, 2/15]
[ 2/9,  2/11,  2/13,  2/15, 2/17]
[2/11,  2/13,  2/15,  2/17, 2/19]
```

```
>> [V, E] = eig (A)
```

V =

```
[ -.1612e-1, -.6740e-2,    .3578,     2.482,   -288.7]
[    .2084,    .1400,   -2.513,    -15.01,    2298.]
[   -.7456,   -.6391,    3.482,     20.13,   -3755.]
[       1,        1,        1,         1,        1]
[   -.4499,   -.5011,   -2.476,    -8.914,    1903.]
```

E =

```
[ 2/55*.4005e-4,            0,             0,            0,            0]
[           0, 2/55* .3991e-2,             0,            0,            0]
[           0,            0, 2/55* .1629,             0,            0]
[           0,            0,             0, 2/55* 3.420,            0]
[           0,            0,             0,            0, 2/55* 34.16]
```

As is well known, the eigenvectors are the columns of the matrix *V* and the eigenvalues are the elements of the diagonal of the matrix *E*.

```
>> pretty(simple(poly(A)))
```

```
 5   10042  4    362807509088  3    268537284608   2
X  - ----- X  + ------------- X  - --------------- X
      7315       2228304933855      285965799844725

         22809860374528              4359738368
    + -------------------- X - -----------------------
      169975437532179654375    1776243322211277388821875
```

We can approximate the above output as follows:

```
>> pretty(simple(vpa(poly(A))))
```

```
      5         4         3          2          -6            -12
    x -1.373 x +.1628 x -.0009391 x +.1342*10   x -.1934*10
```

The singular values are calculated in the following way:

>> pretty (simple (svd (A)))

```
                    [          -5]
                    [.1456*10   ]
                    [           ]
                    [ .0001451  ]
                    [           ]
                    [ .005923   ]
                    [           ]
                    [   .1244   ]
                    [           ]
                    [   1.242   ]
```

The minimal polynomial and the characteristic matrix are calculated in the following way:

>> pretty(simple(sym(maple('minpoly(matrix(5,5,(i,j)-> 1/(i+j-1/2)),x)'))))

```
      34359738368              22809860374528            268537284608     2
- ----------------------- + --------------------- x - --------------- x
  177624332221127738821875   169975437532179654375    285965799844725

      362807509088   3   10042   4    5
  + ------------- x  - ----- x  + x
    2228304933855       7315
```

>> pretty(simple(sym(vpa(maple('minpoly(matrix(5,5,(i,j)->1/(i+j-1/2)),x)')))))

```
           -12             -6            2            3          4    5
  -.1934 10     + .1342 10    x - .0009391 x  + .1628 x  - 1.373 x  + x
```

>> pretty(simple(sym(maple('charmat(matrix(5,5,(i,j)-> 1/(i+j-1/2)),x)'))))

```
        [                                              -2  ]
        [x - 2/3    -2/5        -2/7       -2/9         --  ]
        [                                              11  ]
        [                                                  ]
        [                                    -2        -2  ]
        [ -2/5     x - 2/7      -2/9         --        --  ]
        [                                    11        13  ]
        [                                                  ]
        [                                    -2        -2  ]
        [ -2/7      -2/9      x - 2/11        --        --  ]
        [                                    13        15  ]
        [                                                  ]
        [           -2         -2                       -2  ]
        [ -2/9      --         --        x - 2/15       --  ]
        [           11         13                       17  ]
        [                                                  ]
        [  -2       -2         -2         -2               ]
        [  --       --         --         --      x - 2/19]
        [  11       13         15         17               ]
```

The vector of condition numbers of the eigenvalues is calculated by:

```
>> condeig (numeric (A))
```

ans =

    1.0000
    1.0000
    1.0000
    1.0000
    1.0000

In a more complete way, we can calculate the matrix V whose columns are the eigenvectors of A, the diagonal matrix D whose diagonal elements are the eigenvalues of A, and the vector S of condition numbers of the eigenvalues of A, by using the command:

```
>> [V,D,s] = condeig(numeric(A))
```

V =

0.0102	0.0697	0.2756	-0.6523	0.7026
-0.1430	-0.4815	-0.7052	0.1593	0.4744
0.5396	0.6251	-0.2064	0.3790	0.3629
-0.7526	0.2922	0.2523	0.4442	0.2954
0.3490	-0.5359	0.5661	0.4563	0.2496

D =

0.0000	0	0	0	0
0	0.0001	0	0	0
0	0	0.0059	0	0
0	0	0	0.1244	0
0	0	0	0	1.2423

s =

    1.0000
    1.0000
    1.0000
    1.0000
    1.0000

Using the command *definite*, we find that the matrix A is positive definite:

```
>> maple('definite(matrix(5,5,(i,j)-> 1/(i+j-1/2)),positive_def)')
```

ans =

true

2.4 Matrix Decomposition

MATLAB enables commands that allow you to decompose a matrix as a product of orthogonal matrices and diagonal matrices.

We have already seen how the command *[U, S, V] = svd (A)* returns a diagonal matrix *S* of singular values of *A* (in decreasing order of magnitude), and orthogonal matrices *U* and *V* such that = *U * S * V'*.

We have also seen that you can obtain the Jordan decomposition of a square matrix *A* via the command *[V, J] = jordan (A)*, which returns the Jordan canonical matrix *J* of *A* with the eigenvalues of *A* on its diagonal and the similarity transform *V* whose columns are the eigenvectors of *A*, so that $V^{-1} * A * V = J$.

On the other hand, we have also seen that you can obtain a decomposition of a square matrix *A* via the command Schur, *[U, T] = schur(A)*, which returns an array *T* and an orthogonal matrix *U* such that *A= U * T * U'* and *U'* *U = eye (U)*. If *A* is complex, *T* is an upper triangular matrix with the eigenvalues of *A* on its diagonal. For real *A*, the matrix *T* has real eigenvalues of *A* on its diagonal and complex eigenvalues in *2×2* diagonal blocks in *T*.

We can also find the Hessenberg decomposition of the matrix *A* via the command *[H, P] = hess (A)*, which gives the orthogonal matrix *P* and Hessenberg matrix *H* such that *A= P * H * P'* and *P'* *P = eye (size (P))*.

In addition, MATLAB has a number of other commands for the numeric and symbolic decomposition of a matrix. They include the following:

[L, U] = lu (A) Decomposes the matrix *A* as the product *A = L * U* (an LU decomposition), where *U* is an upper triangular matrix and *L* is a permutation of a lower triangular matrix.

[L, U, P] = lu(A) Returns the lower triangular matrix *L*, the upper triangular matrix *U* and the permutation matrix *P* such that *P *A = L * U*.

R = chol(A) Returns the upper triangular matrix *R* such that *R'* *R =A* (a Cholesky decomposition), where *A* is positive. If *A* is not positive, an error is returned.

[Q, R] =qr (A) Returns the upper triangular matrix *R* of the same dimension as *A*, and the orthogonal matrix *Q* such that *A = Q * R* (a QR decomposition). This decomposition can be applied to non-square matrices.

[Q, R, E] = qr(A) Returns the upper triangular matrix *R* of the same dimension as *A*, the matrix permutation *E* and the orthogonal matrix *Q* such that *A * E = Q * R*.

X = pinv(A) Returns the matrix *X* (the pseudo-inverse of *A*), of the same dimension as *A'* such that *A * X * A = A* and *X * A * X = X*, where *A * X* and *X * A* are hermitian.

In addition, the commands listed below allow the decomposition of both numeric and symbolic matrices. All of these commands must be preceded by the command *maple*.

LUdecomp(A,P='p',L='l',U='u',U1='u1',R='r') decomposes the matrix *A* into the product *A = evalm(P&*L&*U)* (LU decomposition), where U is an upper triangular matrix, *L* is a lower triangular matrix and *P* is a pivot factor. In addition, *U = evalm(U1&*R)* with *U1* upper triangular and *R* a row reduced factor, so that *A = evalm(P&*L&*U1*R)*.

cholesky(A) returns the lower triangular matrix *R* such that *A = evalm(R&*R')* (Cholesky decomposition of *A*). *A* must be positive definite.

QRdecomp(A,Q='q') returns the upper triangular matrix *R* of the same dimension as *A*, and the orthonormal matrix *Q* such that *A = evalm(Q&*R)* (QR decomposition of *A*).

companion(poli,var) gives the matrix *C* associated with the given monic polynomial in the specified variable. If *poly = a0 + a1x +...+x^n*, *C(i,n)=-coeff(poli,var,i-1)*, *i=1...n*, *C(i,i-1)=1*, *i=2...n, and* C(i, j) = 0 for the rest of the elements in the matrix.

frobenius (A) or ratform (A) returns the canonical Frobenius form *F* of the matrix *A*. *F* is a block diagonal matrix *(F = diag(C1,C2,...,Cn))*, where the *Ci* are the companion matrices associated to polynomials *p1, p2,..., pk* such that p_i divides $p_{i-1,}$ *i = 2... K.*

frobenius(A,'P') assigns to *P* the transformation matrix corresponding to the Frobenius form of the matrix *A*, so that evalm $(P^{-1} \& *A \& *P) = F.$

smith(A,var) computes the Smith normal form of a matrix with univariate polynomial entries in var over the integers.

smith(A,var,U,V) in addition returns the matrices *U* and *V* such that *S = evalm(U&*A&*V).*

ismith(A,var) gives the diagonal matrix corresponding to the Smith normal form *S* of the square matrix *A* of polynomials in the variable *var.*

ismith(A,var,U,V) in addition returns the matrices *U* and *V* such that *S = evalm(U&*A&*V).*

hermite(A,var) computes the Hermite normal form (reduced row echelon form) of a matrix *A* of univariate polynomials in var.

hermite(A,var,U) in addition returns the matrix *U* such that *H = evalm(U&*A).*

ihermite(A,var) computes the Hermite normal form (reduced row echelon form) of a matrix *A* of univariate polynomials in var over the integers.

ihermite(A,var,U) in addition returns the matrix *U* such that *H = evalm(U&*A).*

gaussjord (A) returns an upper triangular matrix corresponding to the row reduced (Gauss-Jordan) echelon form of the matrix *A*. This is used to facilitate the solution of systems of linear equations whose coefficient matrix is the matrix *A*.

gaussjord (A, j) returns the j-th column of the above matrix.

gaussjord(A,r,d) gives the row reduced echelon form of the matrix *A*, assigns to the variable *r* the rank of *A* and to the variable *d* the determinant of *submatrix(A,1..r,1..r).* This subarray is used for solving systems of linear equations whose coefficient matrix is *A*.

gausselim (A) performs Gaussian elimination with row pivoting on *A*, returning the reduced matrix. This is used to facilitate the solution of systems of linear equations whose coefficient matrix is the matrix *A*.

gausselim (A, j) returns the j-th column of the row reduced matrix of *A*.

gausselim(A,r,d) returns the row reduced matrix of *A*, assigns the variable *r* to the rank of *A*, and the variable *d* to the determinant of *submatrix(A, 1..r,1..r)* . This subarray is used for solving systems of linear equations whose coefficient matrix is *A*.

backsub (A) returns the vector *x* such that *A *x = V*, where *V* is the last column of the matrix *A*. If *A* is the result of applying forward Gaussian elimination to the augmented matrix of a system of linear equations (via gausselim or gaussjord, for example), backsub completes the solution by back substitution.

backsub (A, V) returns the vector *x* such that *A *x = V.*

backsub(A,V,t) returns the vector *x* such that A * x = V, where the parameter *t* is used for a possible family of parametric solutions of the system.

forwardsub(A,V) returns the vector x such that $A * x = V$. If A is the result of applying Gaussian elimination to the matrix of a system of linear equations (via LUdecomp, for example), forwardsub completes the solution by forward substitution.

forwardsub(A,V,t) returns the matrix X such that $A * X = V$, where the parameter t is used for a possible family of parametric solutions of the system.

forwardsub (A) returns the vector x such that $A * x = V$, where V is the last column of A.

forwardsub(A,B) returns the matrix X such that $A * X = B$.

geneqns(A,[x1,...,xn]) generates a system of linear equations in the given variables, equating each to zero, where the coefficients are determined by the matrix A.

geneqns(A,[x1,...,xn],V) generates a system of linear equations in the given variables, where the right-hand sides of the equations are determined by the vector V and the coefficients are determined by the matrix A.

genmatrix([equation1,...,equationm],[x1,...,xn]) generates the matrix corresponding to the given linear equations with respect to the specified variables.

genmatrix([equation1,...,equationm],[x1,...,xn],flag) generates the matrix corresponding to the given linear equations with respect to the specified variables, including as the last column of the matrix the right-hand sides of the equations.

genmatrix([equation1,...,equationm],[x1,..,xn],name) generates the matrix corresponding to the given linear equations with respect to the specified variables, and assigns a name to the vector that contains the right-hand sides of the equations.

EXERCISE 2-6

Consider the 3×3 matrix A whose rows are given by the vectors (1,5,–2), (–7,3,1) and (2,2,–2). Find the Schur, LU, QR, Cholesky, Hessenberg and singular value decompositions of A. Verify the results. Also find the pseudoinverse of A.

First, we find the Schur decomposition, checking that the result is correct:

```
>> A = [1.5, - 2; - 7, 3, 1; 2,2, - 2];
>> [U, T] = schur (A)

U =

    -0.0530   -0.8892   -0.4544
    -0.9910   -0.0093    0.1337
     0.1231   -0.4573    0.8807

T =

     2.4475   -5.7952   -4.6361
     5.7628    0.3689    2.4332
          0         0   -0.8163
```

Now, we check that $U * T * U' = A$ and that $U * U' = eye\ (3)$:

>> [U * T * U', U * U']

ans =
```
    1.0000    5.0000   -2.0000         1.0000    0.0000    0.0000
   -7.0000    3.0000    1.0000         0.0000    1.0000    0.0000
    2.0000    2.0000   -2.0000         0.0000    0.0000    1.0000
```

Now, we find the LU, QR, Cholesky, Hesenberg and singular value decompositions, checking the results for each case:

>> [L, U, P] = lu (A)

L =
```
    1.0000         0         0
   -0.1429    1.0000         0         Lower triangular matrix
   -0.2857    0.5263    1.0000
```

U =
```
   -7.0000    3.0000    1.0000
         0    5.4286   -1.8571         Upper triangular matrix
         0         0   -0.7368
```
P =
```
    0    1    0
    1    0    0
    0    0    1
```

>> [P * A, L * U]

ans =
```
   -7    3    1   -7    3    1
    1    5   -2    1    5   -2         we have that P*A=L*U
    2    2   -2    2    2   -2
```

>> [Q, R, E] = qr (A)

Q =
```
   -0.1361 - 0.8785 - 0.4579
    0.9526 - 0.2430   0.1831
   -0.2722 - 0.4112   0.8700
```

R =

```
   -7.3485 1.6330 1.7691
    0     -5.9442 2.3366  Upper triangular matrix
    0       0     -0.6410
```

E =
```
    1 0 0
    0 1 0
    0 0 1
```

>> [A * E, Q * R]

ans =

```
    1.0000 5.0000 -2.0000   1.0000 5.0000 -2.0000
   -7.0000 3.0000   1.0000 -7.0000 3.0000   1.0000
    2.0000 2.0000 -2.0000   2.0000 2.0000 -2.0000
```

Then, A * E = Q * R.

>> R = chol(A)

??? Error using ==> chol
Matrix must be positive definite.

We obtain an error message because the matrix is not positive definite.

>> [P,H] = hess(A)

P =

```
    1.0000  0       0
    0      -0.9615 0.2747
    0       0.2747 0.9615
```

H =

```
    1.0000 -5.3571 -0.5494
    7.2801  1.8302 -2.0943
    0      -3.0943 -0.8302
```

>> [P*H*P', P'*P]

ans =

```
    1.0000 5.0000 -2.0000 1.0000 0      0
   -7.0000 3.0000   1.0000 0      1.0000 0
    2.0000 2.0000 -2.0000 0      0      1.0000
```

Then, PHP'= A and P'P = I.

>> **[U, S, V] = svd (A)**

U =

```
  -0.1034 -0.8623   0.4957
  -0.9808  0.0056  -0.1949
   0.1653 -0.5064  -0.8463
```

S =

```
  7.8306 0      0
  0      6.2735 0        diagonal matrix
  0      0      0.5700
```

V =

```
   0.9058 -0.3051 0.2940
  -0.3996 -0.8460 0.3530
  -0.1411  0.4372 0.8882
```

>> **U * S * V'**

ans =

```
   1.0000 5.0000 -2.0000
  -7.0000 3.0000  1.0000 therefore USV'= A
   2.0000 2.0000 -2.0000
```

Now, we calculate the pseudoinverse of *A*:
>> **X = pinv (A)**

X =

```
   0.2857 -0.2143 -0.3929
   0.4286 -0.0714 -0.4643
   0.7143 -0.2857 -1.3571
```

>> **[A * X * A, X * A * X]**

ans =

```
   1.0000 5.0000 -2.0000 0.2857 -0.2143 -0.3929
  -7.0000 3.0000  1.0000 0.4286 -0.0714 -0.4643
   2.0000 2.0000 -2.0000 0.7143 -0.2857 -1.3571
```

Thus, we have *AXA = A* and *XAX = X*.

EXERCISE 2-7

Consider the square matrix of order 5 whose (i, j)th element is defined by Aij = 1/(i+j-1/2). Calculate its Jordan form (and check the result). Find its LU, QR, Frobenius, Smith and Hermite decompositions, calculating the matrices involved and verifying that they do indeed yield the original matrix.

>> **A=sym(maple('matrix(5,5,(i,j)-> i+j-1/2)'))**

A =

```
[3/2, 5/2, 7/2, 9/2, 11/2]
[5/2, 7/2, 9/2, 11/2, 13/2]
[7/2, 9/2, 11/2, 13/2, 15/2]
[9/2, 11/2, 13/2, 15/2, 17/2]
[11/2, 13/2, 15/2, 17/2, 19/2]
```

>> **[V, J] = Jordan (A);**
>> **pretty(sym(V))**

```
    [                     1/2                     1/2              22       19]
    [8/9, 9/170 17 + 3/10,       9/170 3/17 +  3/10,             --,       --]
    [                                                             45       45]
    [                                                                        ]
    [-71              1/2                1/2                       -7         ]
    [---, - 2/85 17 + 1/5,       2/85 17 + 1/5,                  ---  - 2/9]
    [90                                                          18         ]
    [                                                                        ]
    [-67              1/2                1/2                      -49      -14]
    [---, 1/170 17 + 1/10,       -1/170 17 + 1/10,             ----,     ---]
    [90                                                         90        45]
    [                                                                        ]
    [                 1/2                1/2                                  ]
    [3/10, 3/85 17,              - 3/85 17,                    3/10, - 2/5]
    [                                                                        ]
    [31      11   1/2               11    1/2                   -13      -23]
    [-- ,   --- 17    - 1/10 ,   - --- 17  - 1/10 ,            -- ,      --]
    [90     170                    170                         90        45]
```

>> **pretty(sym(J))**

```
    [0             0                   0           0   0]
    [                                                  ]
    [                1/2                                ]
    [0  55/4 + 15/4 17               0           0   0]
    [                                                  ]
    [                                1/2               ]
    [0             0         55/4-15/4 17        0   0]
    [                                                  ]
    [0             0                   0         0   0]
    [                                                  ]
    [0             0                   0         0   0]
```

```
>> pretty(simple(sym(symmul(symmul(V,J),inv(V)))))
```

$$
\begin{bmatrix}
3/2 & 5/2 & 7/2 & 9/2 & 11/2 \\
5/2 & 7/2 & 9/2 & 11/2 & 13/2 \\
7/2 & 9/2 & 11/2 & 13/2 & 15/2 \\
9/2 & 11/2 & 13/2 & 15/2 & 17/2 \\
13/2 & 11/2 & 15/2 & 17/2 & 19/2
\end{bmatrix}
$$

We have calculated the transformation matrix *V* and the diagonal matrix (the Jordan form) *J* of *A*. We have also proven that *V * J * V-1 = A*. We now calculate the LU decomposition matrix of *A* and the matrices involved, checking the result. Since symbolic matrices are involved, we will use the *maple* command.

```
>> maple('A:=matrix(5,5,(i,j)-> i+j-1/2)');
>> pretty (sym (maple ('LUdecomp(A,P=p,L=l,U=u,U1=u1,R=r)')))
```

$$
\begin{bmatrix}
3/2 & 5/2 & 7/2 & 9/2 & 11/2 \\
0 & -2/3 & -4/3 & -2 & -8/3 \\
0 & 0 & 0 & 0 & 0 \\
0 & 0 & 0 & 0 & 0 \\
0 & 0 & 0 & 0 & 0
\end{bmatrix}
$$

```
>> pretty(sym(maple('print(p,l)')))
```

$$
\begin{bmatrix}
1 & 0 & 0 & 0 & 0 \\
0 & 1 & 0 & 0 & 0 \\
0 & 0 & 1 & 0 & 0 \\
0 & 0 & 0 & 1 & 0 \\
0 & 0 & 0 & 0 & 1
\end{bmatrix},
\begin{bmatrix}
1 & 0 & 0 & 0 & 0 \\
5/3 & 1 & 0 & 0 & 0 \\
7/3 & 2 & 1 & 0 & 0 \\
3 & 3 & 0 & 1 & 0 \\
11/3 & 4 & 0 & 0 & 1
\end{bmatrix}
$$

```
>> pretty(sym(maple('print(u1,r)')))
```

$$
\begin{bmatrix}
3/2 & 5/2 & 0 & 0 & 0 \\
0 & -2/3 & 0 & 0 & 0 \\
0 & 0 & 1 & 0 & 0 \\
0 & 0 & 0 & 1 & 0 \\
0 & 0 & 0 & 0 & 1
\end{bmatrix},
\begin{bmatrix}
1 & 0 & -1 & -2 & -3 \\
0 & 1 & 2 & 3 & 4 \\
0 & 0 & 0 & 0 & 0 \\
0 & 0 & 0 & 0 & 0 \\
0 & 0 & 0 & 0 & 0
\end{bmatrix}
$$

```
>> pretty (sym (maple ('evalm(p&*l&*u1&*r), evalm(p&*l&*u)')))
```

```
[3/2   5/2   7/2   9/2   11/2]   [3/2 5/2 7/2 9/2    11/2]
[                            ]   [                       ]
[5/2   7/2   9/2  11/2  13/2]   [5/2 7/2 9/2 11/2   13/2]
[                            ]   [                       ]
[7/2   9/2  11/2 13/2  15/2],   [7/2 9/2 11/2 13/2  15/2]
[                            ]   [                       ]
[9/2  11/2 13/2 17/2  15/2]   [9/2 11/2 13/2 17/2  15/2]
[                            ]   [                       ]
[13/2 11/2 15/2 17/2 19/2]   [13/2 11/2 15/2 17/2 19/2]
```

We see that $p * l * u1 * r = A$ and that $p * l * u = A$. We will then calculate the QR decomposition of A and the matrices involved, checking the result.

```
>> pretty(sym(maple('print(R)')))
```

```
      [      1/2 71     1/2       85     1/2      33    1/2 113    1/2]
      [1/2 285,  --- 285,       --- 285,       --- 285,  --- 285   ]
      [         114            114            38        114         ]
      [                                                            ]
      [               1/2             1/2           1/2        1/2]
      [0,       2/57 570,      4/57 570,     2/19 570,   8/57 570   ]
      [                                                            ]
      [0 ,           0 ,           0 ,          0 ,          0]
      [                                                            ]
      [0 ,           0 ,           0 ,          0 ,          0]
      [                                                            ]
      [0 ,           0 ,           0 ,          0 ,          0]
```

```
>> pretty(sym(maple('print(q)')))
```

```
      [       1/2           1/2          1/2                      ]
      [1/95 285,    3/95 570,    1/5/10,          0,            0]

      [       1/2   11   1/2        1/2        1/2               ]
      [1/57 285,     --- 570,  - 1/5 10,    1/10 30,            0]
      [            570                                          ]

      [       1/2         1/2        1/2        1/2          1/2 ]
      [7/285 285, 2/285 570,     - 1/10, - 2/15 30,        1/6 6   ]

      [       1/2         1/2                  1/2          1/2  ]
      [3/95 285, - 1/190 570,        0, - 1/30 30,       - 1/3 6    ]

      [ 11     1/2         1/2        1/2        1/2           1/2]
      [--- 285 , - 1/57 570,   1/10/10,    1/15 30,         1/6 6    ]
      [285                                                      ]
```

```
>> pretty(sym(maple('evalm(q&*R)')))
```

$$
\begin{bmatrix}
3/2 & 5/2 & 7/2 & 9/2 & 11/2 \\
5/2 & 7/2 & 9/2 & 11/2 & 13/2 \\
7/2 & 9/2 & 11/2 & 13/2 & 15/2 \\
9/2 & 11/2 & 13/2 & 17/2 & 15/2 \\
13/2 & 11/2 & 15/2 & 17/2 & 19/2
\end{bmatrix}
$$

We see that $q * R = A$. Next we find the Smith decomposition of the matrix A and the matrices involved, checking the result.

```
>> pretty(sym(maple('smith(A,X,U,V)')))
```

$$
\begin{bmatrix}
1 & 0 & 0 & 0 & 0 \\
0 & 1 & 0 & 0 & 0 \\
0 & 0 & 0 & 0 & 0 \\
0 & 0 & 0 & 0 & 0 \\
0 & 0 & 0 & 0 & 0
\end{bmatrix}
$$

```
>> pretty(sym(maple('print(U,V)')))
```

$$
\begin{bmatrix}
0 & 0 & 0 & 0 & 2/11 \\
0 & 0 & 0 & 11/2 & -9/2 \\
-1 & 2 & -1 & 0 & 0 \\
0 & 1 & -2 & 1 & 0 \\
0 & 0 & 1 & -2 & 1
\end{bmatrix},
\begin{bmatrix}
1 & \dfrac{-13}{11} & 1 & 2 & 3 \\
0 & 1 & -2 & -3 & -4 \\
0 & 0 & 1 & 0 & 0 \\
0 & 0 & 0 & 1 & 0 \\
0 & 0 & 0 & 0 & 1
\end{bmatrix}
$$

```
>> pretty(sym(maple('evalm(U&*A&*V)')))
```

$$
\begin{bmatrix}
1 & 0 & 0 & 0 & 0 \\
0 & 1 & 0 & 0 & 0 \\
0 & 0 & 0 & 0 & 0 \\
0 & 0 & 0 & 0 & 0 \\
0 & 0 & 0 & 0 & 0
\end{bmatrix}
$$

We see that $U * A * V = $ *Smith matrix*. Next we calculate the Hermite decomposition of the matrix A and find the matrices involved.

```
>> pretty(sym(maple('H:=hermite(A,x,V); V:=evalm(V)')))
>> pretty(sym(maple('print(H,V)')))
```

$$
\begin{bmatrix} 1 & 0 & -1 & -2 & -3 \\ 0 & 1 & 2 & 3 & 4 \\ 0 & 0 & 0 & 0 & 0 \\ 0 & 0 & 0 & 0 & 0 \\ 0 & 0 & 0 & 0 & 0 \end{bmatrix}, \begin{bmatrix} -7/2 & 5/2 & 0 & 0 & 0 \\ 5/2 & -3/2 & 0 & 0 & 0 \\ 2 & -4 & 2 & 0 & 0 \\ 4 & -6 & 0 & 2 & 0 \\ 6 & -8 & 0 & 0 & 2 \end{bmatrix}
$$

```
>> pretty(sym(maple('evalm(V&*A)')))
```

$$
\begin{bmatrix} 1 & 0 & -1 & -2 & -3 \\ 0 & 1 & 2 & 3 & 4 \\ 0 & 0 & 0 & 0 & 0 \\ 0 & 0 & 0 & 0 & 0 \\ 0 & 0 & 0 & 0 & 0 \end{bmatrix}
$$

We see that $V *A = H$. Finally, we calculate the Frobenius decomposition of A and find the matrices involved, checking the result.

```
>> pretty(sym(maple('F:=frobenius(A,P); P:=evalm(P)')))
>> pretty(sym(maple('print(F,P)')))
```

$$
\begin{bmatrix} 0 & 0 & 0 & 0 & 0 \\ 1 & 0 & 50 & 0 & 0 \\ 0 & 1 & 55/2 & 0 & 0 \\ 0 & 0 & 0 & 0 & 0 \\ 0 & 0 & 0 & 0 & 0 \end{bmatrix},
\begin{bmatrix} \dfrac{67}{45} & 3/2 & 285/4 & \dfrac{22}{45} & \dfrac{19}{45} \\ \dfrac{-7}{18} & 5/2 & 355/4 & \dfrac{-7}{18} & -2/9 \\ \dfrac{-49}{90} & 7/2 & 425/4 & \dfrac{-49}{90} & \dfrac{-14}{45} \\ 3/10 & 9/2 & 495/4 & 3/10 & -2/5 \\ \dfrac{13}{90} & 11/2 & 565/4 & \dfrac{13}{90} & \dfrac{23}{45} \end{bmatrix}
$$

```
>> pretty(sym(maple('evalm(P^(-1)&*A&*P)')))
```

$$
\begin{bmatrix}
0 & 0 & 0 & 0 & 0 \\
1 & 0 & 50 & 0 & 0 \\
55/2 & 1 & 0 & 0 & 0 \\
0 & 0 & 0 & 0 & 0 \\
0 & 0 & 0 & 0 & 0
\end{bmatrix}
$$

We have shown that $P-1*A*P = F$.

EXERCISE 2-8

Consider the 3×3 matrix A whose rows are given by the vectors (1,5,–2), (–7,3,1) and (2,2,–2). If V is the vector of ones, solve the system L * x = V based on the LU decomposition of A. Solve the system G * x = V, where G is obtained from A via Gaussian elimination. Solve the system J * x = V where J is the Jordan form of A. Represent the matrix system in the form of equations, and find the Hermite and Smith decompositions of A.

First, we define the matrix *A* and the vector *V* using the *maple* command as follows:

```
>> maple ('A: = matrix(3,3,[1,5,-2,-7,3,1,2,2,-2]);) V: = array ([1,1,1])');
```

Then we find the LU decomposition of *A*, solving the system $L*x = V$ using the command *backsub*.

```
>> pretty(sym(maple('L:=LUdecomp(A)')))
>> pretty(sym(maple('backsub(L,V)')))
```

$$
\begin{bmatrix}
253 & -233 & -19 \\
--- & ---- & --- \\
532 & 532 & 14
\end{bmatrix}
$$

We have solved the system $L *x = V$, which can be expressed in the form of equations with the command *geneqns* as follows:

```
>> pretty(sym(maple('geneqns(L,[x1,x2,x3],V)')))
```

$$
\{x\ 1 + 5\ x\ 2 - 2\ x\ 3 = 1,\ 38\ x\ 2 - 13\ x\ 3 = 1,\ -\frac{14}{19}\ x\ 3 = 1\}
$$

Now we solve the system $G * x = V$ where G is obtained from A by Gaussian elimination.

```
>> pretty(sym(maple('G:=gausselim(A)')))
>> pretty(sym(maple('backsub(G,V)')))
```

$$
\begin{bmatrix}
79 & -11 & \\
-- & --- & -2/7 \\
56 & 56 &
\end{bmatrix}
$$

The system of equations is found as follows:

```
>> pretty(sym(maple('geneqns(G,[x1,x2,x3],V)')))
```

$$\{x\ 1 + 5\ x\ 2 - 2\ x\ 3 = 1,\ 8\ x\ 2 + 2\ x\ 3 = 1,\ -\ 7/2\ x\ 3 = 1\}$$

Now, we solve the system $J * x = V$ where J is the canonical Jordan form of A. We use the command *forwardsub*.

```
>> pretty(sym(maple('J:=gaussjord(A)')))
>> pretty(sym(maple('forwardsub(J,V)')))
```

$$[1\ 1\ 1]$$

Finally, we find the Smith and Hermite matrices associated with A.

```
>> pretty(sym(maple('ihermite(A,x)')))
```

$$
\begin{bmatrix}
1 & 1 & 6 \\
0 & 2 & 3 \\
0 & 0 & 14
\end{bmatrix}
$$

```
>> pretty(sym(maple('ismith(A)')))
```

$$
\begin{bmatrix}
1 & 0 & 0 \\
0 & 1 & 0 \\
0 & 0 & 28
\end{bmatrix}
$$

2.5 Equivalent Matrices and Diagonalization

Two matrices A and B of dimensions $(M \times N)$ are equivalent if there exist two invertible matrices U and V such that $A = UBV$. The MATLAB command $[U, S, V] = svd (A)$ calculates a diagonal matrix S which is equivalent to A.

Two square matrices A and B of order n are said to be congruent if there is an invertible matrix P such that $A = P^tBP$.

The MATLAB command $[U, T] = schur (A)$ calculates a matrix T which is congruent with A.

Congruence implies equivalence, and two congruent matrices must always have the same rank.

Two square matrices of order n, A and B, are similar if there is an invertible matrix P such that $A = PBP^{-1}$. Two similar matrices are equivalent.

A matrix A is diagonalizable if it is similar to a diagonal matrix D, that is, if there is an invertible matrix P such that $A = PDP^{-1}$.

The process of calculating the diagonal matrix D and the matrix P is called diagonalization of A.

Given a square matrix of real numbers A of order n, if all the eigenvalues of A are real and distinct, then A is diagonalizable. The matrix D will have the eigenvalues of A as the diagonal elements. The matrix P has as columns the eigenvectors of A corresponding to these eigenvalues.

If the matrix A has an eigenvalue with multiplicity r greater than 1, then it is diagonalizable if and only if the kernel of the matrix $A - r * I_n$ has dimension equal to the degree of multiplicity of the eigenvalue r.

The MATLAB command $[V, J] = jordan(A)$ diagonalizes the matrix A by calculating the diagonal matrix J and the matrix V such that $A = VJV^{-1}$.

EXERCISE 2-9

Diagonalize the symmetric matrix whose rows are the vectors:

(3,–1,0), (–1,2–1), (0,–1,3).

Check the result and confirm that the eigenvalues of the initial matrix are the elements of the diagonal matrix obtained.

We calculate the diagonal matrix J similar to A, which will have the eigenvalues of A on its diagonal, and the transformation matrix V. To do this, we use the command $[V, J] = jordan(A)$:

```
>> A = [3, -1, 0; -1, 2, -1; 0, -1, 3]

A =

     3  -1   0
    -1  -2  -1
     0  -1   3
```

```
>> [V, J] = jordan (A)

V =

[1/6,   1/2,  1/3]
[1/3,   0,   -1/3]
[1/6,  -1/2,  1/3]

J =

[1, 0, 0]
[0, 3, 0]
[0, 0, 4]
```

We now confirm that the diagonal matrix J has the eigenvalues of A on its diagonal:

```
>> eigensys (A)

ans =

[1]
[3]
[4]
```

The matrices *A* and *J* are similar because there a matrix *V* satisfying the equation *V-1* * *A* * *V* = *J* :

```
>> symmul(symmul(inv(V),A),V)
```

ans =

```
[1, 0, 0]
[0, 3, 0]
[0, 0, 4]
```

2.6 Sparse Matrices

A matrix is called sparse if it has sufficiently many zero elements that one can take advantage of. Sparse matrix algorithms do not store most null elements in memory, so when working on matrix processing with sparse matrices one gains time and efficiency. There are specialized commands that can be used to deal with sparse matrices. Some of these commands are listed below.

S = sparse (i, j, s, m, n, nzmax), i = vector, j = vector, s = vector. Creates a sparse matrix S of dimension *m×n* with space for *nzmax* non-zero elements given by s. The vector *i* contains the i-input components of the non-null elements and the vector *j* contains the corresponding j-input components.

S=sparse(i,j,s,m,n). Creates the sparse matrix S using *nzmax=length(s)*.

S = sparse(i,j,s). Creates a sparse matrix S with *m = max (i)* and *n = max (j)*.

S = sparse (A) converts the matrix A into sparse form.

A = full (S) converts the sparse matrix S into full matrix form A.

S = spconvert (D) converts an external ASCII file read with name *D* into a sparse matrix S.

(i, j) = find (A) returns the row and column indices of the non-zero entries of the matrix A.

B = spdiags (A, d) builds a sparse matrix by extracting the diagonal elements of A specified by the vector d.

S = speye (m, n) creates the sparse *m×n* matrix with ones on the main diagonal.

S = speye (n) creates the sparse square identity matrix of order *n*.

R = sprandn (S) generates a random sparse matrix with non-zero values normally distributed in (0,1) with the same structure as the sparse matrix S.

R = sprandsym (S) generates a sparse random symmetric matrix with non-zero entries normally distributed in (0,1) whose lower diagonal triangle has the same structure as S.

r = sprank (S) gives the structural rank of the sparse matrix S.

n = nnz (S) gives the number of non-zero elements in the sparse matrix S.

k = nzmax (S) returns the amount of storage occupied by the non-zero elements in the sparse matrix S. If S is a full matrix then *nzmax (S) = prod (size (S))*.

s=spalloc(m,n,nzmax) creates space in memory for a sparse matrix of dimension *m×n*.

R = spones (S) replaces the zero entries of the sparse matrix S with ones.

n = condest (S) computes a lower bound for the 1-norm condition number of a square matrix S.

m = normest (S) returns an estimate of the 2-norm of the matrix S.

issparse (A) returns 1 if the matrix *A* is sparse, and 0 otherwise.

Here are some examples:

>> **sparse([1,1,2,2,3,4],[4,2,3,1,2,3],[-7,12,25,1,-6,8],4,4,10)**

ans =

```
(2,1) 1
(1,2) 12
(3,2) -6
(2,3) 25
(4,3) 8
(1,4) -7
```

Now we convert this sparse matrix into complete form:

>> **full (ans)**

ans =

```
0   12  0  -7
1    0 25   0
0   -6  0   0
0    0  8   0
```

Now we define a sparse matrix whose full form is a diagonal matrix:

>> **sparse(1:5,1:5,-6)**

ans =

```
(1,1)     -6
(2,2)     -6
(3,3)     -6
(4,4)     -6
(5,5)     -6
```

>> **full(ans)**

ans =

```
-6   0   0   0   0
 0  -6   0   0   0
 0   0  -6   0   0
 0   0   0  -6   0
 0   0   0   0  -6
```

2.6.1 Special Matrices

MATLAB provides commands to define certain special types of matrices. These include the following:

H = hadamard(n): Returns the Hadamard matrix of order n, a matrix with values 1 or - 1 such that $H'^* H = n * eye(n)$.

hankel(V): Returns the square Hankel matrix whose first column is the vector V and whose elements are zero below the first anti-diagonal. The matrix $hankel(C,R)$ has first column vector C and last row vector R.

hilb(n): Returns the Hilbert matrix of order n, a matrix whose ij-th element is $1/(i+j-1)$.

invhilb(n): Returns the inverse of the Hilbert matrix of order n.

magic(n): Returns a magic square of order n. Its elements are integers from 1 to n^2 with equal sums of rows and columns.

pascal(n): Returns the Pascal matrix of order n (symmetric, positive definite with integer entries taken from Pascal's triangle).

rosser: Returns the Rosser matrix, an 8 x 8 matrix with a double eigenvalue, three nearly equal eigenvalues, dominant eigenvalues of the opposite sign, a zero eigenvalue and a small non-zero eigenvalue.

toeplitz(C,R): Returns a Toeplitz matrix (not symmetric, with the vector C in the first column and R as the first row vector).

vander(C): Returns a Vandermonde matrix whose penultimate column is the vector C. In addition, $A(:,j) = C \wedge (n-j)$.

wilkinson(n): Returns the Wilkinson matrix of order n (symmetric tridiagonal with pairs of eigenvalues close but not the same).

compan(P): Returns the corresponding companion matrix whose first row is -P(2:n)/P(1), where P is a vector of polynomial coefficients.

maple('hadamard (n)'): Returns the Hadamard matrix of order n, a matrix with values 1 or - 1 such that $H'^* H = n * eye(n)$.

maple ('hilbert (n)'): Returns the Hilbert matrix of order n, a matrix whose ij-th element is $1/(i+j-1)$.

maple ('hilbert(n,exp)')Returns the matrix of order n with ij-th entry equal to $1/(i+j-exp)$.

maple('bezout(poly1,poly2,x)'): Constructs the Bézout matrix of the given polynomials in x, with dimension $max(m,n)$, where $m = degree (poly1)$ and $n = degree (poly2)$. The determinant of this matrix is the resultant of the two polynomials $(resultant(poly1,poly2,x))$.

maple('sylvester(p1,p2,x)'): Constructs the Sylvester matrix of the given polynomials in x, with dimension $n+m$, where $m = degree(p1)$ and $n = degree(p2)$. The determinant of this matrix is the resultant of the two polynomials.

maple ('fibonacci (n)'): Returns the nth Fibonacci matrix F(n) whose size is the sum of the dimensions of F (n-1) and F (n-2).

maple('toeplitz([ex1,...,exn])'): Returns the symmetric Toeplitz matrix whose elements are the specified expressions.

maple('vandermonde([expr1,..., exprn])'): Returns the Vandermonde matrix whose ij-th element is expri^{j-1}.

maple ('wronskian(V,x)') Returns the Wronskian matrix of the vector V =(f1,...,fn) with respect to the variable *x*. The ij-th element is *diff (fj, x$(i-1))*.

maple ('jacobian([expr1,...,exprm],[x1,..., xn])'): Returns the *mxn* Jacobian matrix with ij-th element *diff(expri,xj)*.

maple('hessian(exp,[x1,...,xn])'): Returns the *mxn* Hessian matrix with ij-th element *diff(exp, xi,xj)*.

EXERCISE 2-10

Find the eigenvalues of the Wilkinson matrix of order 8, a magic square of order 8 and the Rosser matrix.

```
>> [eig(wilkinson(8)), eig(rosser), eig(magic(8))]
```

ans =

  1. 0e + 003 *

0.0042	1.0000	0.2600
0.0043	1.0000	0.0518
0.0028	1.0200	-0.0518
0.0026	1.0200	0.0000
0.0017	1.0199	0.0000 + 0.0000i
0,0011	0.0001	0.0000 - 0.0000i
0.0002	0.0000	0.0000 + 0.0000i
-0.0010	-1.0200	0.0000 - 0.0000i

Observe that the Wilkinson matrix has pairs of eigenvalues which are close, but not equal. The Rosser matrix has a double eigenvalue, three nearly equal eigenvalues, dominant eigenvalues of the opposite sign, a zero eigenvalue and a small non-zero eigenvalue.

EXERCISE 2-11

Find the Smith and Hermite forms of the inverse of the Hilbert matrix of order 2 in the variable x. Also find the corresponding transformation matrices.

```
>> maple('with(linalg):H:= inverse(hilbert(2,x))');
>> pretty(simple(sym(maple('H'))))
```

$$
\begin{bmatrix}
-(-3+x)^2 (-2+x) & (-3+x)(-2+x)(-4+x) \\
(-3+x)(-2+x)(-4+x) & -(-3+x)^2 (-4+x)
\end{bmatrix}
$$

```
>> maple ('B: = smith(H,x,U,V);)U: = eval (U); V: = eval (V)');
>> pretty(simple(sym(maple('B'))))
```

$$
\begin{bmatrix}
-3+x & 0 \\
0 & (-2+x)(x^2 - 7x + 12)
\end{bmatrix}
$$

```
>> pretty(simple(sym(maple('U'))))
```

$$
\begin{bmatrix}
-1 & -1 \\
10 - 13/2\, x + x^2 & -13/2\, x + 9 + x^2
\end{bmatrix}
$$

```
>> pretty(simple(sym(maple('V'))))
```

$$
\begin{bmatrix}
-7/2 + x & -4 + x \\
-3/2 + x & -2 + x
\end{bmatrix}
$$

```
>> maple('HM:=hermite(H,x,Q);Q:=evalm(Q)');
>> pretty(simple(sym(maple('HM'))))
```

$$
\begin{bmatrix}
x^2 - 5x + 6 & 0 \\
0 & x^2 - 7x + 12
\end{bmatrix}
$$

```
>> pretty(simple(sym(maple('Q'))))
```

$$
\begin{bmatrix}
-x+3 & -x+2 \\
-x+4 & -x+3
\end{bmatrix}
$$

EXERCISE 2-12

Verify that the functions x, x^2 and x^3 are linearly independent.

```
>> maple('v:=[x,x^2,x^3]:w:=wronskian(v,x)');
>> pretty(simple(sym(maple('w'))))
```

$$
\begin{bmatrix}
x & x^2 & x^3 \\
1 & 2x & 3x^2 \\
0 & 2 & 6x
\end{bmatrix}
$$

```
>> pretty(simple(sym(maple('det(w)'))))
```

$$2 x^3$$

Since the determinant of the Wronskian is non-zero, the functions are linearly independent.

EXERCISE 2-13

Find the Jacobian matrix and the Jacobian determinant of the transformation:

x = e u sin (v), y = e u cos (v).
```
>> pretty (sym (maple ('jacobian (vector ([exp (u) * sin (v), exp (u) * cos (v)]),
[u, v])')))
```

$$
\begin{bmatrix}
exp\ (u)\ sin\ (u) & exp\ (u)\ cos\ (v) \\
exp\ (u)\ cos\ (v) & -\ exp\ (u)\ sin\ (v)
\end{bmatrix}
$$

```
>> pretty(simple(sym(maple('det(")'))))
```

$$-exp\ (u)^2$$

EXERCISE 2-14

Find the Bézout and Sylvester matrices B and T for the functions $p = a + bx + cx^2$ and $q = d + ex + fx^2$. Verify that the determinants of B and T coincide with the resultant of p and q.

```
>> maple('p:=a+b*x+c*x^2; q:= d+e*x+f*x^2; B:=bezout(p, q, x); T:=sylvester(p, q, x)')
>> pretty(sym(maple('B')))
```

$$
\begin{bmatrix} dc - af & db - ae \\ & \\ ec - bf & dc - af \end{bmatrix}
$$

```
>> pretty(sym(maple('T')))
```

$$
\begin{bmatrix} c & b & a & 0 \\ 0 & c & b & a \\ f & e & d & 0 \\ 0 & f & e & d \end{bmatrix}
$$

```
>> pretty(sym(maple('det(B)'))),pretty(sym(maple('det(T)'))),
pretty(sym(maple('resultant(p,q,x)')))
```

$$
d^2 c^2 - 2\,d\,c\,a\,f + a^2 f^2 - d\,b\,y\,c + d\,b^2 f + a\,e^2 c - a\,e\,b\,f
$$

$$
d^2 c^2 - 2\,d\,c\,a\,f + a^2 f^2 - d\,b\,y\,c + d\,b^2 f + a\,e^2 c - a\,e\,b\,f
$$

$$
d^2 c^2 - 2\,d\,c\,a\,f + a^2 f^2 - d\,b\,y\,c + d\,b^2 f + a\,e^2 c - a\,e\,b\,f
$$

CHAPTER 3

■ ■ ■

Sequences, Arrays, Tables, Lists and Sets

This chapter covers such essential mathematical concepts as strings, arrays, and tables, which allow for fluid work in vector and matrix analysis, and also the treatment of all kinds of sums and products, both finite and infinite. MATLAB also implements sets and lists. For all of these concepts, we first present the definitions and then give a summary of the commands that can be used to implement them in MATLAB.

3.1 Sequences

A sequence is simply an ordered list of items separated by commas. As well as presenting a sequence explicitly, separating the elements with commas, one can also use the $ operator to create sequences. In particular, lists and sets are represented externally by sequences of elements between square brackets and braces respectively. The string of length zero is valid in MATLAB and is assigned the special name **NULL**. Among the commands that enable MATLAB to handle sequences (all of which must be preceded by the **maple** command) we have the following:

> **seq (f (i), i = a...b) creates the sequence $f(a), f(a+1),..., f(b-1), f(b)$. The numbers a and b must be integers.**

> **seq(expr,var=a..b) creates the sequence of expressions resulting from the substitution of the variable *var* into the expression *expr* where var ranges over the values a, $a+1$,..., $b-1$, b. The numbers a and b must be integers.**

> **seq (f(i), i = expr) creates the sequence corresponding to the values of f applied to the expression *expr*.**

> **seq (f(i), i = list) creates the sequence corresponding to the values obtained by applying the function f to the elements of the specified list.**

> **seq (f(i), i = set) creates the sequence corresponding to the values obtained by applying the function f to elements of the specified set.**

> **f (i) \$ i = a...b creates the sequence $f(a), f(a+1),..., f(b-1), f(b)$. The numbers a and b need not be integers.**

> **\$ a..b creates the sequence, $a+1, a+2,..., b-1, b$. The numbers a and b need not be integers.**

> **f \$ n creates the sequence $f, f,.............f$ (with n occurrences of f).**

> **s [i] returns the ith element of the sequence s.**

nops ([s]) gives the length of the string *s* (number of elements).

op (list) returns the sequence formed by the elements of the specified list.

op (set) returns the sequence formed by the elements of the specified set.

[s] creates the list whose elements are those of the sequence *s*.

{s} creates the set whose elements are those of the sequence *s*.

s,s creates a sequence formed by the repetition of the sequence *s*.

s, s,..., s (n occurrences of *s*) creates a sequence formed by the repetition of the sequence *s* n times.

sequence: = NULL defines the empty sequence.

add(expr, var=a..b) sums the sequence of expressions obtained by substituting the values *a, a+1,..., b-1, b* of the variable *var* into the expression *expr*.

add (f (i), i = a...b) sums the sequence $f(a), f(a+1),..., f(b-1), f(b)$. The values *a* and *b* must be numeric.

add (f (i), i = expr) adds the sequence of numerical values obtained by applying *f* to the expression *expr*.

add (f (i), i = list) adds the sequence of values obtained when applying the function *f* to the elements from the specified list.

add (f (i), i = set) adds the sequence of values obtained by applying the function *f* to the elements of the given set.

mul(expr, var=a..b) finds the product of the sequence of expressions obtained by substituting the values *a, a+1,..., b-1, b* of the variable *var* into the expression *expr*.

mul(f (i), i = a...b) finds the product of the sequence $f(a), f(a+1),..., f(b-1), f(b)$. The values *a* and *b* must be numeric.

mul(f (i), i = expr) finds the product of the sequence of numerical values obtained by applying *f* to the expression *expr*.

mul(f (i), i = list) finds the product of the sequence of values obtained by applying the function *f* to the elements of the given list.

mul(f (i), i = set) finds the product of the sequence of values obtained by applying the function *f* to the elements of the given set.

sum(expr, var=a..b) finds the sum of the sequence of expressions obtained by substituting the values *a, a+1,..., b-1, b* of the variable *var* into the expression *expr*. The values *a* and *b* can be symbolic.

sum (f (i), i = a...b) finds the sum of the sequence $f(a), f(a+1),..., f(b-1), f(b)$. That is, it returns the sum $\sum_{i=a}^{b} f(i)$. The values *a* and *b* can be symbolic.

product(expr, var=a..b) finds the product of the sequence of expressions obtained by substituting the values *a, a+1,..., b-1, b* of the variable *var* into the expression *expr*.

product (f (i), i = a...b) finds the product of the sequence $f(a), f(a+1),..., f(b-1), f(b)$. That is, it returns the product $\sum_{i=a}^{b} f(i)$. The values *a* and *b* can be symbolic.

op(a..b, expr) or seq(op(i,expr), i=a..b) extracts the sequence comprising the a-th through b-th operands of the expression *expr*.

Here are some examples:

```
>> pretty (sym (maple('mul(k, k=1..5)')))
```

$$120$$

```
>> pretty(sym(maple('add( k^2, k=1..5 )')))
```

$$55$$

```
>> pretty(sym(maple('L:= [seq(k, k=1..5)] '))),pretty(sym(maple('L')))
```

$$\begin{bmatrix} 1 & 2 & 3 & 4 & 5 \end{bmatrix}$$

```
>> pretty(sym(maple('add( k^2, k=L)')))
```

$$55$$

```
>> pretty(sym(maple('mul( x-k, k=L ) ')))
```

$$(x - 1)\ (x - 2)\ (x - 3)\ (x - 4)\ (x - 5)$$

```
>> pretty(sym(maple('add( a[k]*x^k, k=0..5 ) ')))
```

$$a[0] + a[1]\ x + a[2]\ x^2 + a[3]\ x^3 + a[4]\ x^4 + a[5]\ x^5$$

```
>> pretty(sym(maple('add( k^2, k=0..n ) ')))
```

$$\textit{Error, unable to execute add}$$

This example failed because n is a symbolic value. You will need to use the command *sum*.

```
>> pretty(sym(maple('sum( k^2, k=0..n ) ')))
```

$$1/3\ (n + 1)^3 - 1/2\ (n + 1)^2 + 1/6\ n + 1/6$$

```
>> pretty(sym(maple('product( k^2, k=1..4 ) ')))
```

$$576$$

```
>> pretty(sym(maple('mul( k^2, k=1..4 ) ')))
```

$$576$$

```
>> pretty(sym(maple('product( k^2, k=1..n ) ')))
```

$$gamma(n + 1)^2$$

```
>> pretty(sym(maple('product( k^2, k ) ')))
```

$$gamma(k)^2$$

```
>> pretty(sym(maple('product( a[k], k=0..4 ) ')))
```

$$a[0]\ a[1]\ a[2]\ a[3]\ a[4]$$

```
>> pretty(sym(maple('seq( k^2, k=1..5 ) ')))
```

$$1,\ 4,\ 9,\ 16,\ 25$$

```
>> pretty(sym(maple('seq( sin(Pi*k/6), k=0..6 ) ')))
```

$$0,\ 1/2,\ 1/2\ 3^{1/2},\ 1,\ 1/2\ 3^{1/2},\ 1/2,\ 0$$

```
>> pretty(sym(maple('seq( x[k], k=1..5 ) ')))
```

$$x[1],\ x[2],\ x[3],\ x[4],\ x[5]$$

```
>> pretty(sym(maple('product( a[k], k=0..n ) ')))
```

```
>> pretty(sym(maple('sum(a[k]*x^k,k=0..n) ')))
```

$$\sum_{k=0}^{n}\ a[k]\ x^{k}$$

```
>> pretty(sym(maple('sum(k/(k+1), k=0..n)')))
```

$$n + 1 - Psi(n + 2) - eulergamma$$

```
>> pretty(sym(maple('sum(k/(k+1), k)')))
```

$$k - Psi(k + 1)$$

```
>> pretty(sym(maple('$ 2..5')))
```

$$2, \ 3, \ 4, \ 5$$

```
>> pretty(sym(maple('k^2 $ k = 2/3 .. 8/3')))
```

$$4/9, \ 25/9, \ 64/9$$

```
>> pretty(sym(maple('a[k] $ k = 1..3')))
```

$$a[1], \ a[2], \ a[3]$$

```
>> pretty(sym(maple('x$4')))
```

$$x, \ x, \ x, \ x$$

```
>> pretty(sym(maple('u:= [1,4,9]:')));
>> pretty(sym(maple('nops(u)')))
```

$$3$$

```
>> pretty(sym(maple('op(2,u)')))
```

$$4$$

```
>> pretty(sym(maple('op(2..3,u)')))
```

$$4, \ 9$$

EXERCISE 3-1

Generate the list containing the sequence of integers from zero to six. Generate the list containing the sequence of its squares and the set containing the sequence of its squares modulo seven. Also generate the list whose elements are pairs of values where the first element of the pairs run through the integers from zero to six, and the second element is the square of the first.

```
>> maple('X:= [seq( k, k=0..6 )] ')
```

ans =

X: = [0, 1, 2, 3, 4, 5, 6]

```
>> maple('Y:= [seq(k^2, k=X)] ')
```

ans =

Y: = [0, 1, 4, 9, 16, 25, 36]

```
>> maple('{seq(k^2 mod 7, k=X)} ')
```

ans =

{0, 1, 2, 4}

```
>> maple ('[seq ([X [k], Y [k]], k = 1.. nops (X))] ')
```

ans =

[[0, 0], [1, 1], [2, 4], [3, 9], [4, 16], [5, 25], [6, 36]]

EXERCISE 3-2

Generate the sequence of 1st through 10th derivatives of the function ln (x). Generate another sequence of 15 random numbers between 5 and 50.

```
>> pretty (sym (maple ('seq (diff (ln (x), x$ n), n = 1.. 10)')))
```

$$1/x, \ -\frac{1}{x^2}, \ \frac{2}{x^3}, \ -\frac{6}{x^4}, \ \frac{24}{x^5}, \ -\frac{120}{x^6}, \ \frac{720}{x^7}, \ -\frac{5040}{x^8}, \ \frac{40320}{x^9}, \ -\frac{362880}{x^{10}}$$

```
>> pretty(sym(maple('f:=rand(5..50):seq(f( ),k=1..15)')))
```

30, 5, 42, 24, 17, 39, 48, 9, 28, 42, 18, 8, 50, 29, 7

EXERCISE 3-3

Calculate the following sums and product:

$$\sum_{n\geq1} ne^{-n}, \ \sum_{k=0}^{23} \frac{(1+i)^k}{(\pi+k)^5}, \ \text{and} \ \prod_{n=1}^{10} n^2 \frac{2^n}{e^n}.$$

```
>> pretty(sym(maple('sum(n*E^(-n),n=1..infinity) ')))
```

$$\frac{E}{(-1 + E)^2}$$

```
>> pretty(sym(maple('evalf(sum((1+i)^k/(Pi+k)^5,k=0..23)) ')))
```

.003599764471 +.001081437031 I

This value, with numerical summation limits, can also be found with the command *add* as follows:

```
>> pretty(sym(maple('evalf(add((1+I)^k/(Pi+k)^5,k=0..23))')))
```

$$.003599764471 + .001081437031\ i$$

```
>> pretty(sym(maple('evalf(product(n^2*2^n/exp(n),n=1..10))')))
```

$$616565.6460$$

With numerical limits, this product can also be found using the command *mul* as follows:

```
>> pretty(sym(maple('evalf(mul(n^2*2^n/exp(n),n=1..10)) ')))
```

$$616565.6460$$

EXERCISE 3-4

Calculate the following sums: $\sum_{k=1}^{n} k^3$, $\sum_{k=1}^{n} k^4$ and $\sum_{k=1}^{n} k^5$

```
>> pretty (sym (maple('sum(k^3, k=0..n) ')))
```

$$1/4\ (n + 1)^4\ -\ 1/2\ (n + 1)^3\ +\ 1/4\ (n + 1)^2$$

```
>> pretty(sym(maple('sum( k^4, k=0..n ) ')))
```

$$1/5\ (n + 1)^5\ -\ 1/2\ (n + 1)^4\ +\ 1/3\ (n + 1)^3\ -\ 1/30\ n\ -\ 1/30$$

```
>> pretty(sym(maple('sum( k^5, k=0..n ) ')))
```

$$1/6\ (n + 1)^6 - 1/2\ (n + 1)^5\ +\ 5/12\ (n + 1)^4 - 1/12\ (n + 1)^2$$

3.2 Arrays

An array is a well-ordered collection of individual elements each of which is associated with a (possible multi-) index which indicates its position in the array. It is essential that each element is associated with a unique index, which may also be zero or negative, so that, in order to make changes to any element of the array, one simply refers to its index.

Arrays can be of one or more dimensions, so an array may have one or more sets of indices that identify its elements. The most important commands that enables MATLAB to work with arrays are as follows (all of them must be preceded by the *maple* command):

array(1..n, element_list) creates the array with *n* elements specified in the list and whose indices vary from 1 to *n*.

array (n..m, item_list) creates the array with the *m-n + 1* elements specified in the list and whose indices vary from *n* to *m*.

array(1..n) creates an array with *n* unspecified elements whose indices vary from 1 to *n*.

array (n..m) creates the array with *m-n + 1* unspecified elements whose indices vary from *n* to *m*.

array (item_list) creates an array whose elements are taken from the list (of length n) and whose indices vary from 1 to *n*.

array(1..m, 1..n, [list1,...,listn]) creates a two-dimensional array of *n* rows and *m* columns, where the rows of elements are the given lists. The indices are the pairs (i, j) with i = 1... n, j = 1... m.

array(1..m, 1..n, 1..p, [[list11,...,list1n],...[listm1,...,listmn]],...,

[[listp1,...,listpn],...,[list(p+m)1,...,list(p+m)n]] creates a three-dimensional array whose elements are given by the specified lists. The indices are the triples (i, j, k) with i = 1... n, j = 1.. m, k = 1.. p.

array(1..n, option) or **array(1..n,1..m, option)** creates a one-dimensional or two-dimensional array of the type specified in option. The option values are *symmetric, antisymmetric, diagonal, identity or sparse.*

A [i] returns the element with index i in the one-dimensional array A.

A [i, j] returns the element with index (i, j) in the two-dimensional array A.

A [i]: = *element* assigns the element to the array element with index i.

A [i, j]: = *element* assigns the element to the array element with index (i, j).

eval (array) or **evalm (array)** shows the elements of an array in certain non-trivial cases.

op (eval (array)) shows the internal structure of the array and allows access to its elements.

op (n, eval (array)) extracts the nth operand of the array. The first operand is the index function, the second operand is a sequence of ranges or indices and the third operand is the table of data representing the elements of the array.

nops(array) or **nops(eval(array))** gives the number of elements in the array.

indices(A) shows the indices of the array A.

entries(A) shows the elements of the array A.

copy(A) creates a copy of the array A.

map(function, array) applies the given command or function to all the elements of the array.

subs ({old = new}, eval (array)) replaces the old element with the new throughout the array.

subs ({old1 = new1, old2 = new2,..., oldn = newn}, eval (array)) replaces the old elements with the new throughout the array.

convert(A,list) creates the one-dimensional array corresponding to the given list with the same elements.

convert (A, listlist) converts the two-dimensional array A to a list of lists.

convert (A, vector) converts the one-dimensional array A to a vector with the same elements.

convert(A,matrix) converts the two dimensional array to a matrix.

convert (A set) converts the one-dimensional array A to a set with the same elements.

type(expression, array) determines if the expression is an array.

type(expression, 'array' (type)) determines whether the expression is an array with all the elements of the given type (integer, complex,...).

typematch (expression, array) returns true if the given expression is of type array.

typematch(expr, array, name) in addition, if the match is successful, assigns to *name* a list of equations representing the variables and their matched values.

Here are some examples:

>> **pretty (sym (maple ('array(1..3, 1..3, [[a,b,c],[d,e,f],[g,h,i]])')))**

$$\begin{matrix} [a & b & c] \\ [& &] \\ [d & e & f] \\ [& &] \\ [g & h & i] \end{matrix}$$

>> **pretty(sym(maple('array(3..6,[a,b,c,d]) ')))**

array(3 .. 6, [

    3 = a

    4 = b

    5 = c

    6 = d

    ])

>> **pretty(sym(maple('array(1..2,1..2,identity) ')))**

$$\begin{matrix} [1 & 0] \\ [0 & 1] \end{matrix}$$

```
>> pretty(sym(maple('array(1..2, 1..6, [(1,3)=p, (2,4)=r], sparse) ')))
```

$$
\begin{array}{cccccc}
[0 & 0 & p & 0 & 0 & 0] \\
[& & & & &] \\
[0 & 0 & 0 & r & 0 & 0]
\end{array}
$$

```
>> pretty(sym(maple('M:=array(1..2, 1..3,[[2,8,32], [45,-1,0]]) ')));
>> pretty(sym(maple('M')))
```

$$
\begin{array}{ccc}
[2 & 8 & 32] \\
[& &] \\
[45 & -1 & 0]
\end{array}
$$

```
>> pretty(sym(maple('M[1,3] ')))
```

$$32$$

```
>> pretty(sym(maple('M[2,3]:=x-3 ')));
>> pretty(sym(maple('op(M) ')))
```

$$
\begin{array}{ccc}
[2 & 8 & 32] \\
[& &] \\
[45 & -1 & x - 3]
\end{array}
$$

```
>> pretty(sym(maple(' v:= array(1..4): ')));
>> pretty(sym(maple('for k to 3 do v[k]:= k^2 od: ')))
>> pretty(sym(maple('print(v) ')))
```

$$[1, 4, 9, v[4]]$$

```
>> pretty(sym(maple('v[2] ')))
```

$$4$$

```
>> pretty(sym(maple('v[0] ')))
```

Error, 1st index, 0, smaller than lower array bound 1

```
>> pretty(sym(maple('A:= array(1..2,1..2): ')));
>> pretty(sym(maple('A[1,2]:= x ')));
>> pretty(sym(maple('print(A) ')))
```

$$
\begin{array}{cc}
[A[1, 1] & x] \\
[&] \\
[A[2, 1] & A[2, 2]]
\end{array}
$$

```
>> pretty(sym(maple('A:= array( symmetric, 1..2,1..2, [ [1,x], [x,x^2] ] ) ')))
>> pretty(sym(maple('A')))
```

$$
\begin{array}{cc}
[1 & x] \\
[&] \\
[& 2] \\
[x & x]
\end{array}
$$

```
>> pretty(sym(maple('op(A)')))
```

$$
\begin{bmatrix}
1 & x \\
& \\
& 2 \\
x & x
\end{bmatrix}
$$

```
>> pretty(sym(maple('op(1,eval(A)) ')))
```

$$symmetric$$

```
>> pretty(sym(maple('op(2,eval(A)) ')))
```

$$1 \;..\; 2, \; 1 \;..\; 2$$

```
>> pretty(sym(maple('op(3,eval(A)) ')))
```

$$[(1,\, 2) = x, \; (1,\, 1) = 1, \; (2,\, 2) = x^2]$$

```
>> pretty(sym(maple('map(diff,A,x) ')))
```

$$
\begin{bmatrix}
0 & 1 \\
& \\
1 & 2\,x
\end{bmatrix}
$$

EXERCISE 3-5

Generate a one-dimensional array with three elements whose indices range from 1 to 3 and fill the array with the squares of the first three natural numbers. Also generate a two-dimensional array whose two indices vary from 1 to 3 and fill the array with ones in the first row, the squares of the first three positive integers in the second row and the cubes of the first three positive integers in the third row. Finally, replace all ones in the two-dimensional array by fives and check the result. Convert the first array to a set and the second to a list.

```
>> pretty (sym (maple (' squ: = array(1..3) ')));
>> maple('squ[1]:=1^2;squ[2]:=2^2;squ[3]:=3^2 ');
>> pretty(sym(maple('print(squ) ')))
```

$$[1,\, 4,\, 9]$$

```
>> pretty(sym(maple('bidimen:=array(1..3,1..3) ')));
>> maple('bidimen[1,1]:=1;bidimen[1,2]:=1;bidimen[1,3]:=1;
   bidimen[2,1]:=1^2;bidimen[2,2]:=2^2;bidimen[2,3]:=3^2;
   bidimen[3,1]:=1^3;bidimen[3,2]:=2^3;bidimen[3,3]:=3^3 ');
```

>> **pretty(sym(maple('print(bidimen)')))**

$$\begin{array}{ccc} [1 & 1 & 1] \\ [& &] \\ [1 & 4 & 9] \\ [& &] \\ [1 & 8 & 27] \end{array}$$

>> **pretty(sym(maple('subs({1=5}, evalm(bidimen)) ')))**

$$\begin{array}{ccc} [5 & 5 & 5] \\ [& &] \\ [5 & 4 & 9] \\ [& &] \\ [5 & 8 & 27] \end{array}$$

A more elegant way to define the two arrays of this problem is as follows:

>> **pretty(sym(maple('squ:=array(1..3,[seq(k^2,k=1..3)]) ')))**

$$[1 \quad 4 \quad 9]$$

>> **pretty(sym(maple('bidimen:=array(1..3,1..3,[[seq(k^0,k=1..3)],**
   [seq(k^2,k=1..3)],[seq(k^3,k=1..3)]]) ')))
>> **pretty(sym(maple('bidimen')))**

$$\begin{array}{ccc} [1 & 1 & 1] \\ [& &] \\ [1 & 4 & 9] \\ [& &] \\ [1 & 8 & 27] \end{array}$$

>> **pretty(sym(maple('convert(squ,set) ')))**

$$\{1, 4, 9\}$$

>> **pretty(sym(maple('convert(bidimen,listlist) ')))**

$$[[1, 1, 1], [1, 4, 9], [1, 9 , 27]]$$

EXERCISE 3-6

Generate a three-dimensional array containing the first eight positive natural numbers and whose three indices vary from 1 to 2. Access its operands and display its internal structure.

```
>> pretty(sym(maple('tridimen:=array(1..2,1..2,1..2,[[[1,2],[3,4]],[[5,6],[7,8]]])')))
>> pretty(sym(maple('tridimen')))
```

array(1 .. 2, 1 .. 2, 1 .. 2, [

    (1, 1, 1) = 1

    (1, 1, 2) = 2

    (1, 2, 1) = 3

    (1, 2, 2) = 4

    (2, 1, 1) = 5

    (2, 1, 2) = 6

    (2, 2, 1) = 7

    (2, 2, 2) = 8

    ])

```
>> pretty(sym(maple('op(eval(tridimen)) ')))
```

[1 .. 2, 1 .. 2, 1 .. 2], [(1, 1, 1) = 1, (1, 1, 2)= 2, (1, 2, 1)= 3,

(1, 2, 2)=4, (2, 1, 1)=5, (2, 1, 2) = 6, (2, 2, 1) = 7, (2, 2, 2) = 8]

```
>> pretty(sym(maple('op(1,eval(tridimen)) ')))
```

                [1 .. 2   1 .. 2   1 .. 2]

```
>> pretty(sym(maple('op(2,eval(tridimen)) ')))
```

  [(1, 1, 1) = 1 (1, 1, 2) = 2, (1, 2, 1) = 3, (1, 2, 2) = 4,]

  (2, 1, 1) = 5, (2, 1, 2) = 6, (2, 2, 1) = 7 (2, 2, 2) = 8]

3.3 Relationships Between Vectors, Matrices and Arrays

A vector is equivalent to a one-dimensional array whose index begins with 1. Therefore, a vector is a special case of an array. As we know, MATLAB defines a vector with m row elements in the following ways:

> **maple('array([v1, ..., vm])')**

> **maple ('vector(m, item_list)')**

> **maple ('vector([v1,..., vm])')**

> **maple ('vector (m, k - > f (k))')**

Here are some examples:

```
>> pretty(sym(maple('vector(4,[1,x,x^2,x^3]) ')))
```

$$[1, x, x^2, x^3]$$

```
>> pretty(sym(maple('vector([1,x,x^2,x^3]) ')))
```

$$[1, x, x^2, x^3]$$

```
>> pretty(sym(maple('array([1,x,x^2,x^3]) ')))
```

$$[1, x, x^2, x^3]$$

```
>> pretty(sym(maple('vector(3,k->k^2)')))
```

$$[1 \quad 4 \quad 9]$$

A matrix is equivalent to a two-dimensional array whose indices both begin at 1. Therefore, a matrix is also a special case of a two-dimensional array. As we know, MATLAB allows you to define an array of dimension $(m{\times}n)$ in the following ways:

> **maple ('matrix([lista1,..., listam])')** (each list has n elements and is a row of the matrix)

> **maple ('array([lista1,..., listam])')** (each list has n elements and is a row of the matrix)

> **maple ('matrix (m, n, item_list)')**

> **maple('matrix(m, n, (i,j)->f(i,j))')**

Here are some examples:

```
>> pretty (sym (maple ('matrix ([[sin(x), x^2 + x + 3], [exp (x), cos(x^2)]])')))
```

$$\begin{bmatrix} \sin(x) & x^2 + x + 3 \\ \exp(x) & \cos(x)^2 \end{bmatrix}$$

```
>> pretty(sym(maple('array([[sin(x), x^2+x+3], [exp(x), cos(x^2)]])')))
```

$$
\begin{bmatrix}
\sin(x) & x^2 + x + 3 \\
\exp(x) & \cos(x^2)
\end{bmatrix}
$$

```
>> pretty (sym (maple ('matrix (2,2, [sin (x), x ^ 2 + x + 3, exp (x), cos(x^2)])')))
```

$$
\begin{bmatrix}
\sin(x) & x^2 + x + 3 \\
\exp(x) & \cos(x^2)
\end{bmatrix}
$$

```
>> pretty(sym(maple('matrix(3,4,(p,q)->a^p+b^q)')))
```

$$
\begin{bmatrix}
a + b & a + b^2 & a + b^3 & a + b^4 \\
a^2 + b & a^2 + b^2 & a^2 + b^3 & a^2 + b^4 \\
a^3 + b & a^3 + b^2 & a^3 + b^3 & a^3 + b^4
\end{bmatrix}
$$

On the other hand, we know that by using the command *convert* we can transform any one-dimensional array to a vector and any two-dimensional array to a matrix.

3.3.1 Tables

The concept of a table is an extension of the concept of an array. The difference between an array and a table is that the indices of a table need not vary over integers. For example, you can build a table with algebraic formulas as indices and their derivatives as values in the table. Therefore, the table structure is much more powerful that the array structure. Let's look at the most common MATLAB commands that enable you to work with tables (all of them must be preceded by the *maple* command):

> **table ([(index1) = element1,..., (indexn) = elementn]) creates a table with the specified indices and elements (inputs).**

> **table([element1,...,elementn]) creates a table with the specified elements which have indices 1, 2,..., n.**

> **table (option, [(index1) = element1,..., (indexn) = elementn]) creates a table of the type specified by the option *(symmetric, antisymmetric, diagonal, identity or sparse)* with the given indices and elements.**

> **T [i] returns the element of index *i* of the table T.**

> **T [i]: = *element* assigns the element to the entry of T with index i.**

> **eval (table) or evalm (table) shows the elements of a table in certain non-trivial cases.**

op (eval (table)) shows the internal structure of the table and allows access to its elements.

op (n, eval (table)) extracts the nth operand of the table. The first operand is the index function and the second operand is a list of equations whose left-hand sides are the indices and whose right-hand sides are the elements of the table.

nops (T) or nops (eval (T)) gives the number of elements in the table T.

indexes(T) shows the indices of the table T.

entries (T) shows the elements of the table T.

copy (T) creates a copy of the table T.

map (function, table) applies the given command or function given to all the elements of the array.

subs ({old = new}, eval (table)) replaces the old element with the new throughout the table.

subs ({old1 = new1, old2 = new2,..., oldn = newn}, eval (table)) replaces the old items for new ones throughout the table.

convert(T,list, '=') converts the table T to a list of equations of the form index T = element.

convert(T,multiset) converts the table T to a list of lists such that the first elements are the indices of the table T and the second elements are their corresponding values.

convert(T,set) converts the table T to a set containing the elements of the table, ignoring the indices.

type(expression, table) determines if the expression is a table.

type (expression, 'table' (type)) determines whether the expression is a table with elements of the given type (integer, complex...).

typematch (expression, table) returns true if the given expression is of type table.

typematch (expr, array, name) in addition, if the match is successful, assigns to name a list of equations representing the variables and their matched values.

Here are some examples:

```
>> pretty (sym (maple ('table ()')))
```

table([
*   ])*

```
>> pretty(sym(maple('table([22,42]) ')))
```

table([
*   1 = 22*
*   2 = 42*
*   ])*

```
>> pretty(sym(maple('S:= table([(2)=45,(4)=61]) ')))
>> pretty(sym(maple('S')))
```

S:= table([
 2 = 45
 4 = 61
    ])

```
>> pretty(sym(maple('T:= table(symmetric,[(c,b)=x]) ')))
>> pretty(sym(maple('T')))
```

T:= table(symmetric, [
    (c, b) = x
    ])

```
>> pretty(sym(maple('op(T) ')))
```

table(symmetric, [
    (c, b) = x
    ])

```
>> pretty(sym(maple('F:= table([sin=cos,cos=-sin]): ')))
>> pretty(sym(maple('op(F) ')))
```

table([)
    cos = - sin
    sin = cos
    ])

```
>> pretty(sym(maple('op(2,eval(F)) ')))
```

$$[cos = - sin, \; sin = cos]$$

```
>> pretty (sym (maple ('op (op (F))')))
```

$$[cos = - sin, \; sin = cos]$$

```
>> pretty (sym (maple ('F [cos](Pi/2) ')))
```

$$-1$$

```
>> pretty(sym(maple('convert(F,set) ')))
```

$$\{cos, \; -sin\}$$

```
>> pretty(sym(maple('convert(F,multiset) ')))
```

$$[[cos,-sin], \; [sin, \; cos]]$$

3.5 Lists

As we know, a list is a collection of objects separated by commas and enclosed within square brackets. It is a sequence enclosed within square brackets. The order of the elements in a list is important, and elements can be repeated, i.e. the lists [a, b, c] and [b, c, a] are different, and the lists [a, a, b, c, c] and [a, b, c] are also different. The following commands can be used to create and manipulate lists (all must be preceded by the command *maple*):

[a1, a2,..., an]creates a list of the given elements.

[sequence] create a list whose elements are defined in the specified sequence.

list: = [] defines the empty list.

L [i] returns the ith element of the list L.

L[-i] returns the ith element from the end of the list L.

L [a...b] returns the elements of the list that occupy the places a, a+1,..., b-1, b.

L [-a...-b] returns the elements of the list that occupy the places a, a+1,..., b-1, b starting from the end of the list.

[list, list] create a list of two lists.

[list,..., list] creates a list of *n* lists.

member (expression, list) determines whether the expression belongs to the list.

member(expr, list, name) assigns the specified name to the first item in the list that matches *expr*.

nops (L) gives the number of elements in the list L.

op (L) transforms the list L into a sequence.

op (n, L) gives the nth element in the list L.

op(a..b, L) gives the a-th through b-th elements of the list L, inclusive.

convert (A, list) converts the one-dimensional array A into a list.

convert(V,list) converts the vector V into a list.

convert(M, list, list) converts the matrix M into a list of lists.

convert(expression, list) converts the given expression into a list whose first operands are its elements.

convert(T, list, '=') converts the table T into a list of equations of the form index = element.

convert({expr1,..., exprn}, list) converts the set of expressions into a list.

convert (A, listlist) converts the two-dimensional array A into a list of lists.

convert([index1=element1,..., indexn=elementn], listlist) converts the given list of equations into a list that contains only items properly sorted by index, but not the indices themselves.

convert(L, set) converts the list L into a set with the same elements, ignoring indices.

convert(T, multiset) converts the table T into a list of lists such that the first elements are the indices of the table T and the second elements are their corresponding values.

convert([expr1,..., exprn], option) creates a list with the given expressions converted according to the specified option (trig, exp, ln,...).

convert(L,vector) converts the list L to a vector.

convert([list1,..., listn], matrix) converts the list of lists to a matrix whose rows are the given lists.

type (expression, list) determines whether the expression is a list.

type(expresion, listlist) determines whether the expression is a list of lists.

type(expression, 'list' (type)) determines whether the expression is a list with the elements of the given type (integer, complex...).

typematch (expression, list) returns true if the given expression is of type list.

typematch (expr, list, name) in addition, if the match is successful, assigns to *name* a list of equations representing the variables and their matched values.

Here are some examples:

```
>> pretty (sym (maple ('L: = [seq(x[k],k=1..4)] ')))

>> pretty(sym(maple('L')))
```

$$[x[1], \ x[2], \ x[3], \ x[4]]$$

```
>> pretty(sym(maple('L[2]')))
```

$$x[2]$$

```
>> pretty(sym(maple(' L:= [op(L),x[5]] ')))

>> pretty(sym(maple(' L')))
```

$$[x[1], \ x[2], \ x[3], \ x[4], \ x[5]]$$

```
>> pretty(sym(maple('L, L[-3..-2]) ')))
```

$$[x[3], \ x[4]]$$

```
>> pretty (sym (maple ('member(x*y, [x*y, w+u, y])')))
```

$$true$$

```
>> pretty(sym(maple('member(w, [x, y, w, u], k) ')))
```

$$true$$

```
>> pretty(sym(maple('convert( [1,2,3,4], `+` ) ')))
```

$$10$$

```
>> pretty(sym(maple('u:= [1,4,9] ')))
>> pretty(sym(maple('u')))
```

$$[1 \quad 4 \quad 9]$$

```
>> pretty(sym(maple('nops(u) ')))
```

$$3$$

```
>> pretty(sym(maple('op(2,u) ')))
```

$$4$$

```
>> pretty(sym(maple('op(2..3,u) ')))
```

$$4, 9$$

```
>> pretty(sym(maple('op(u) ')))
```

$$1, 4, 9$$

```
>> pretty(sym(maple('op(-1,u) ')))
```

$$9$$

```
>> pretty(sym(maple('op(0,u) ')))
```

$$list$$

```
>> pretty(sym(maple('[op(u),16] ')))
```

$$[1, 4, 9, 16]$$

```
>> pretty(sym(maple('X:= [seq( k, k=0..6 )] ')))
>> pretty(sym(maple('Y:= [seq( k^2, k=X )] ')))
>> pretty(sym(maple('X,Y')))
```

$$\begin{matrix} [0 & 1 & 2 & 3 & 4 & 5 & 6] \\ [0 & 1 & 4 & 9 & 16 & 25 & 36] \end{matrix}$$

```
>> pretty(sym(maple('[seq( [X[k],Y[k]], k=1..nops(X) )] ')))
```

$$[[0, 0], [1, 1], [2, 4], [3, 9], [4, 16], [5, 25], [6, 36]]$$

3.5.1 Selecting and Manipulating Elements From Lists

Among the multiple possibilities for structural handling of lists offered by MATLAB, the following group of commands allows the selection and manipulation of elements from lists:

> **select(boolean_function, list) creates a list by selecting from the specified list the items that match the command or given Boolean function.**

> **select(boolean_function, list, expr1,..., exprn) applies the given Boolean function with parameters *expr1,..., exprn* to the elements of the given list to determine which ones are selected.**

> **remove(boolean_function, list) creates a list by removing from the specified list the items that match the given command or Boolean function.**

> **remove(boolean_function, list, expr1,..., exprn) applies the given Boolean function with parameters *expr1,..., exprn* to the elements of the given list to determine which ones are removed.**

> **zip(function, L1, L2) uses lists or vectors of L1 and L2 to generate a new list whose elements are the result of applying the specified binary function to each pair of corresponding elements of the lists. If the two lists do not have the same length, the process only applies up to the length of the shortest list.**

> **zip(function, L1, L2, expr) as above except the length of the generated list is equal to the length of the longest of the two lists L1 and L2 and any empty elements at the tail of the list are filled with the value given by *expr*.**

Here are some examples:

```
>> pretty (sym (maple ('L: = [8, 2.95, Pi, sin(9)] ')))
>> pretty(sym(maple('L')))
```

$$[8 \quad 2.95 \quad pi \quad sin(9)]$$

```
>> pretty(sym(maple('select(type, L, numeric) ')))
```

$$[8, 2.95]$$

```
>> pretty(sym(maple('f:=x->is(x>3) ')))

>> pretty(sym(maple('select(f,L) ')))
```

$$[8, pi]$$

```
>> pretty(sym(maple('remove(f,L) ')))
```

$$[2.95, sin(9)]$$

```
>> pretty (sym (maple ('zip ((x,y) - > x + y, [1,2,3], [4,5,6]) ')))
```

$$[5, 7, 9]$$

```
>> pretty(sym(maple('zip(gcd,[0,14,8],[2,6,12]) ')))
```

$$[2, \ 2, \ 4]$$

```
>> pretty(sym(maple('zip((x,y)->x+y,[1,2,3],[4,5],0) ')))
```

$$[5, \ 7, \ 3]$$

```
>> pretty(sym(maple('zip((x,y)->x^2+y^2,[a,b,c,d,e],[1,2,3],k) ')))
```

$$[a^2 + 1, \ b^2 + 4, \ c^2 + 9 \ d^2 + k^2, \ e^2 + k^2]$$

EXERCISE 3-7

Generate the list containing the integers between 10 and 30, selecting from it the prime numbers. Obtain a new list by selecting only the even numbers.

```
>> pretty(sym(maple('integers:= [$10..30] ')))
>> pretty(sym(maple('integers')))
```

$$[10 \ , \ 11 \ , \ 12 \ , \ 13 \ , \ 14 \ , \ 15 \ , \ 16 \ , \ 17 \ , \ 18 \ , \ 19 \ , \ 20 \ , \ 21 \ , \ 22 \ , \ 23 \ , \ 24$$

$$, \ 25 \ , \ 26 \ , \ 27 \ , \ 28 \ , \ 29 \ , \ 30]$$

```
>> pretty(sym(maple('select(isprime,integers) ')))
```

$$[11, \ 13, \ 17, \ 19, \ 23, \ 29]$$

```
>> pretty(sym(maple('select(type,integers, even) ')))
```

$$[10, \ 12, \ 14, \ 16, \ 18, \ 20, \ 22, \ 24, \ 26, \ 28, \ 30]$$

EXERCISE 3-8

Let X be the list of the first six primes and let Y be the list of binomial coefficients, 6 choose k, for k from 1 to 6. Construct a list P consisting of ordered pairs such that the first element of P[i] is X[i] and the second element of P[i] is Y[i].

```
>> pretty(sym(maple('X:=[seq(ithprime(k), k=1..6)] ')))
>> pretty(sym(maple('X')))
```

$$[2 \quad 3 \quad 5 \quad 7 \quad 11 \quad 13]$$

```
>> pretty(sym(maple('Y:=[seq(binomial(6,k), k=1..6)] ')))
>> pretty(sym(maple('Y')))
```

$$[6 \quad 15 \quad 20 \quad 15 \quad 6 \quad 1]$$

```
>> pretty(sym(maple('pairs:=(x,y)->[x,y] ')))
>> pretty(sym(maple('P:=zip(pairs,X,Y) ')))
>> pretty (sym (maple ('P')))
```

$$[[2, 6], [3, 15], [5, 20], [7, 15], [11, 6], [13, 1]]$$

3.5.2 Ordering and Applying Functions to Lists

MATLAB includes a group of commands whose purpose is the management of elements of lists. One can also apply functions to items in lists. Commands to this effect are summarized below (all require the prior use of the ***maple*** command):

> **sort (list) or sort (list, lexorder) or sort (list, string): sorts the elements of the given list using lexicographical order.**

> **sort (list, numeric) or sort(list, '<') or sort([num1,..., numn]): sorts the elements of the numerical list in numerical order from least to greatest.**

> **sort (list, boolean_function): sorts the elements of the list according to the values of the specified Boolean function applied to pairs in the list.**

> **sort (list, address): sorts the elements of the given list by internal address.**

> **map (function, list): applies the specified command or function to each item in the list.**

> **map (function, list, expr1,..., exprn): applies the specified command or function (with the parameters *expr1,..., exprn*) to each element from the given list.**

> **map2 (function, expression, list): applies the specified command or function to each element of the list, so that the function takes as its first argument a constant given by the expression and as second argument each item in the list.**

> map2 (function, expression, list, expr3, expr4,..., exprn): applies the command or function to each element of the list in such a way that the function has as its first argument a constant given by the expression, as the second argument each element of the list, and as constant arguments from the third to the nth arguments the expressions *expr3, expr4,..., exprn.*

Here are some examples:

```
>> pretty (sym (maple ('sort ([3,2,1])')))
```

$$[1, 2, 3]$$

```
>> pretty(sym(maple('sort([c,a,d],lexorder)')))
```

$$[a, c, d]$$

```
>> pretty(sym(maple('sort([3.12, 1, 1/2], (x,y)->evalb(x>y))')))
```

$$[3.12, 1, 1/2]$$

```
>> pretty(sym(maple('sort([3.12, 1, 1/2], (x,y)->is(x<y))')))
```

$$[1/2, 1, 3.12]$$

```
>> pretty(sym(maple('sort([Jonas,Jeremias,Jose,Roberto,Andres],
  (x,y)->evalb(length(x)<length(y)) ')))
```

$$[Jose \quad Jonas \quad Andres \quad Roberto \quad Jeremias]$$

```
>> pretty(sym(maple('map(f, [a,b,c])')))
```

$$[f(a), f(b), f(c)]$$

```
>> pretty(sym(maple('map2(f, g, [a,b,c])')))
```

$$[f(g, a), f(g, b), f(g, c)]$$

```
>> pretty(sym(maple('map2(op, 1, [a+b,c+d,e+f])')))
```

$$[a, c, e]$$

```
>> pretty (sym (maple ('map2(diff,x^y/z,[x,y,z])')))
```

$$\left[\frac{x^y \, y}{x \, z}, \frac{x^y \, \ln(x)}{z}, -\frac{x^y \, y}{z^2}\right]$$

```
>> pretty(sym(maple('map(x->x^2,[-1,-2,-3,3,2,1])')))
```

$$[1, 4, 9, 9, 4, 1]$$

3.5.3 Performing Operations With Elements of Lists

There are MATLAB commands that allow you to perform sums and products on elements of lists. Among them are the following (all require the prior use of the command ***maple***):

> **add(expression, variable = list) or add (f (i), i = list) gives the sequence of elements obtained by adding the given expression or function to each element of the list.**

> **mul(expression, variable = list) or add (f (i), i = list) gives the sequence of elements obtained by multiplying each element of the list by the given expression or function.**

> **seq(expression, variable = list) or add (f (i), i = list) gives the sequence of elements obtained by applying the specified expression or function to each element of the list.**

Here are some examples:

```
>> pretty (sym (maple ('L: = [seq(k, k=1..5)] ')))
>> pretty(sym(maple('L')))
```

$$[1 \quad 2 \quad 3 \quad 4 \quad 5]$$

```
>> pretty(sym(maple('add( k^2, k=L ) ')))
```

$$55$$

```
>> pretty(sym(maple('mul( x-k, k=L ) ')))
```

$$(x - 1) \ (x - 2) \ (x - 3) \ (x - 4) \ (x - 5)$$

```
>> pretty(sym(maple('A:=x^3+3*x^2+3+x+1 ')))
>> pretty(sym(maple('seq(degree(k,x),k=A) ')))
```

$$3, \ 2, \ 0, \ 1$$

EXERCISE 3-9

Construct Pascal's triangle of binomial coefficients up to its tenth row.

```
>> pretty(sym(maple('L:=[seq(k, k=0..9)] ')))
>> pretty(sym(maple('L')))
```

$$[0 \quad 1 \quad 2 \quad 3 \quad 4 \quad 5 \quad 6 \quad 7 \quad 8 \quad 9]$$

```
>> pretty(sym(maple('[seq(select(type,[seq(binomial(n,m),m=L)],posint),n=L)] ')))
```

```
[[1], [1, 1], [1, 2, 1], [1, 3, 3, 1], [1, 4, 6, 4, 1],
[1, 5, 10, 10, 5, 1], [1, 6, 15, 20, 15, 6, 1],
[1, 7, 21, 35, 35, 21, 7, 1], [1, 8, 28, 56, 70, 56, 28, 8, 1],
[1, 9, 36, 84, 126, 126, 84, 36, 9, 1]]
```

```
>> pretty(sym(maple('map(print,") ')))
```

$$[1]$$

$$[1, \ 1]$$

$$[1, \ 2, \ 1]$$

$$[1, \ 3, \ 3, \ 1]$$

$$[1, \ 4, \ 6, \ 4, \ 1]$$

$$[1, \ 5, \ 10, \ 10, \ 5, \ 1]$$

$$[1, \ 6, \ 15, \ 20, \ 15, \ 6, \ 1]$$

$$[1, \ 7, \ 21, \ 35, \ 35, \ 21, \ 7, \ 1]$$

$$[1, \ 8, \ 28, \ 56, \ 70, \ 56, \ 28, \ 8, \ 1]$$

$$[1, \ 9, \ 36, \ 84, \ 126, \ 126, \ 84, \ 36, \ 9, \ 1]$$

3.5.4 Sets

A set is a collection of objects separated by commas and enclosed in braces. It is a sequence enclosed between braces. The order of the elements in a set is not important and repeating elements will not change the identity of a set, i.e., the sets {a, b, c} and {b, c, a} are equal, and the sets {a, a, b, c, c} and {a, b, c} are also equal. Among the commands relating to sets we have the following (all must be preceded by the command **maple**):

{a1, a2,..., an} creates the set with the specified elements.

{string} creates a set whose elements are defined by the specified string.

set: = {} defines the empty set.

C[i] returns the ith element of the set C.

C[-i] returns the ith element from the end of the set C.

C[a...b] returns the *a*th through *b*th elements of the set C, inclusive.

C[-a...-b] returns the *a*th through *b*th elements from the end of the set C.

[set1, set2] creates an ordered pair of two sets.

[set1,..., setn] creates an ordered n-tuple of sets.

member (expression, C) determines whether the expression belongs to the set C.

member (expr, C, name) assigns the specified name to the first item in the set that matches *expr*.

nops (C) gives the number of elements of the set C.

op (C) converts the sequence C into a set.

op (n, C) gives the nth element of the set C.

op (a..b, C) gives the ath through bth elements of the set C.

convert (A,set) converts a one-dimensional array A to a set.

convert (L, set) converts the list L to a set.

convert (expression, set) converts the given expression to a set whose elements are its first level operands.

convert (T, set) converts the table T to a set containing the elements in the table, ignoring its indices.

convert ([expr1,..., exprn], set) converts the list of expressions to a set.

convert (C,list) converts the set C to a list with the same elements, ignoring indices.

convert ({expr1,..., exprn}, option) creates a set with the given expressions converted according to the specified option (trig, exp, ln,...).

type (expression, set) determines whether the expression is a set.

type (expression, set (type)) determines whether the expression is a set with elements of the given type (integer, complex...).

typematch(expression, set) returns true if the given expression is of type set.

typematch (expr, set, name) in addition, if the match is successful, assigns to name a list of equations representing the variables and their matched values.

select (boolean_function, set) creates a set by selecting the elements of the given set that match the command or Boolean function.

select (boolean_function, set, expr1,..., exprn) applies the Boolean function with the given parameters *expr1,..., exprn* to the elements in the set to determine which ones are selected.

remove (boolean_function, set) creates a set by deleting from the given set the elements that match the given command or Boolean function.

remove (boolean_function, set, expr1,..., exprn) applies the Boolean function with the given parameters *expr1,..., exprn* to the elements in the set to determine which ones are removed.

map (function, C) applies the specified command or function to each element of the set C.

map (function, C, expr1,..., exprn) applies the specified command or function (with the parameters *expr1,..., exprn*) to each element of the set C.

map2 (function, expression, C) applies the specified binary command or function to the pairs with first argument a constant given by the expression and second element each element in the set C, collecting all such values together to form a set.

map2 (function, expression, C, expr3, expr4,..., exprn) applies the specified n-ary command or function with first argument the constant expression, second argument each element of the set C and for third to nth arguments the expressions *expr3, expr4,..., exprn*, collecting all such values together to form a set.

add (expression, variable = set) or add (f(i), i = set) finds the sum of the sequence of elements obtained by applying the specified expression or function to each element in the set.

mul (expression, variable = set) or mul(f(i), i = set) finds the product of the sequence of elements obtained by applying the specified expression or function to each element in the set.

seq (expression, variable = set) or seq (f i), i = set) constructs the sequence of elements obtained by applying the specified expression or function to each element in the set.

C1 union C2 is the set union of the sets C1 and C2.

'union' (C1, C2) is the set union of the sets C1 and C2.

C1 intersect C2 is the set intersection of the sets C1 and C2.

'intersect'(C1, C2) is the set intersection of the sets C1 and C2.

C1 minus C2 is the set difference of the sets C1 and C2.

'minus' (C1, C2) is the set difference of the sets C1 and C2.

readlib (symmdiff): symmdiff (C1, C2, ..., Cn) is the symmetric difference of the specified sets.

Here are some examples:

```
>> pretty(sym (maple(' {x,y,y} ')))
```

$$\{x, \ y\}$$

```
>> pretty(sym(maple(' {y,x,y} ')))
```

$$\{x, \ y\}$$

```
>> pretty(sym (maple('[x,y,y] ')))
```

$$[x, \ y, \ y]$$

```
>> pretty(sym (maple('[y,x,y] ')))
```

$$[y, \ x, \ y]$$

```
>> pretty(sym(maple(' S:= {a,b,c} '))),pretty(sym(maple('S')))
```

$$\{a, \ b, \ c\}$$

```
>> pretty(sym(maple(' S[1] ')))
```

$$a$$

```
>> pretty(sym(maple(' S[1..2] ')))
```

$$\{a, \ b\}$$

```
>> pretty(sym(maple(' S[-2..-1] ')))
```

$$\{b,\ c\}$$

```
>> pretty(sym(maple(' u:= {1,4,9} '))),pretty(sym(maple(' u')))
```

$$\{1,\ 4,\ 9\}$$

```
>> pretty(sym(maple(' nops(u) ')))
```

$$3$$

```
>> pretty(sym(maple(' op(2,u) ')))
```

$$4$$

```
>> pretty(sym(maple(' op(2..3,u) ')))
```

$$4,\ 9$$

```
>> pretty(sym(maple(' op(u) ')))
```

$$1,\ 4,\ 9$$

```
>> pretty(sym(maple(' op(-1,u) ')))
```

$$9$$

```
>> pretty(sym(maple(' op(0,u) ')))
```

$$set$$

```
>> pretty(sym(maple('[op(u),16] ')))
```

$$[1,\ 4,\ 9,\ 16]$$

```
>> pretty(sym(maple(' member(y, {x, y, z}) ')))
```

$$true$$

```
>> pretty(sym(maple(' member(y, {x*y, y*z}) ')))
```

$$false$$

```
>> pretty(sym(maple(' {a,b} union {b,c} ')))
```

$$\{c,\ b,\ a\}$$

```
>> pretty(sym(maple(' {a,b} intersect {b,c} ')))
```

$$\{b\}$$

```
>> pretty(sym(maple(' {a,b} minus {b,c} ')))
```

$$\{a\}$$

```
>> pretty(sym(maple(' a union b union a ')))
```

$$a \ union \ b$$

```
>> pretty(sym(maple(' {3,4} union a union {3,7} ')))
```

$$a \ union \ \{3, \ 4, \ 7\}$$

```
>> pretty(sym(maple(' 'union' ({3,4},a,{3,7}) ')))
```

$$a \ union \ \{3, \ 4, \ 7\}$$

```
>> pretty(sym(maple(' integers:= {$10..20} '))),pretty(sym(maple(' integers')))
```

$$\{10, \ 11, \ 12, \ 13, \ 14, \ 15, \ 16, \ 17, \ 18, \ 19, \ 20\}$$

```
>> pretty(sym(maple(' select(isprime, integers) ')))
```

$$\{11, \ 13, \ 17, \ 19\}$$

```
>> pretty(sym(maple(' remove(isprime, integers) ')))
```

$$\{10, \ 12, \ 14, \ 15, \ 16, \ 18, \ 20\}$$

```
>> pretty(sym(maple(' map(f, {a,b,c}) ')))
```

$$\{f(a), \ f(b), \ f(c)\}$$

```
>> pretty(sym(maple(' map2(f, g, {a,b,c}) ')))
```

$$\{f(g, \ a), \ f(g, \ b), \ f(g, \ c)\}$$

```
>> pretty(sym(maple(' map(proc(x,y) x^2+y end, {1,2,3,4}, 2) ')))
```

$$\{3, \ 6, \ 11, \ 18\}$$

```
>> pretty(sym(maple(' map2(op, 1, {a+b,c+d,e+f}) ')))
```

$$\{a, \ e, \ c\}$$

EXERCISE 3-10

Z1 is the set of integers from 2 to 15. Z2 is the set of primes contained in Z1. Z3 is the set of odd integers contained in Z2 and Z4 is the set of even integers contained in Z2. Calculate the sets: $A = Z2 \cap Z3$, $B = Z2 \cap Z4$, $C = A \cup B$, $E = (A \cup B)\text{-}C$, $F = A \triangle B$, $G = A \triangle B \triangle C$, $H = Z2 \triangle K$ and $Z3 = Z1 \triangle Z2 \triangle Z3$.

```
>> pretty(sym(maple('Z1:={seq(k,k=2..15)} '))),pretty(sym(maple('Z1')))
```

$$\{2, \ 3, \ 4, \ 5, \ 6, \ 7, \ 8, \ 9, \ 10, \ 11, \ 12, \ 13, \ 14, \ 15\}$$

```
>> pretty(sym(maple('Z2:=select(isprime,Z1) '))),pretty(sym(maple('Z2')))
```

$$\{2, \ 3, \ 5, \ 7, \ 11, \ 13\}$$

```
>> pretty(sym(maple('Z3:=select(type,Z2,odd) '))), pretty(sym(maple('Z3')))
```

$$\{3, \ 5, \ 7, \ 11, \ 13\}$$

```
>> pretty(sym(maple('Z4:=select(type,Z2,even)'))),pretty(sym(maple('Z4')))
```

$$\{2\}$$

```
>> pretty(sym(maple(' A:= Z2 intersect Z3 '))),pretty(sym(maple(' A')))
```

$$\{3, \ 5, \ 7, \ 11, \ 13\}$$

```
>> pretty(sym(maple('B:=Z2 intersect Z4 '))),pretty(sym(maple('B')))
```

$$\{2\}$$

```
>> pretty(sym(maple('C:=A union B '))),pretty(sym(maple('C')))
```

$$\{2, \ 3, \ 5, \ 7, \ 11, \ 13\}$$

```
>> pretty(sym(maple('E:=(A union B) minus C '))),pretty(sym(maple('E')))
```

$$[\ ]$$

```
>> pretty(sym(maple( 'readlib(symmdiff): F:=symmdiff(A,B) '))),pretty(sym(maple( 'F')))
```

$$\{2, \ 3, \ 5, \ 7, \ 11, \ 13\}$$

```
>> pretty(sym(maple('G:=symmdiff(A,B,C) '))),pretty(sym(maple('G')))
```

$$[\ ]$$

113

```
>> pretty(sym(maple('H:=symmdiff(Z2,Z3) '))),pretty(sym(maple('H')))
```

$$\{2\}$$

```
>> pretty(sym(maple('K:=symmdiff(Z1,Z2,Z3) '))),pretty(sym(maple('K')))
```

$$\{3, \ 4, \ 5, \ 6, \ 7, \ 8, \ 9, \ 10, \ 11, \ 12, \ 13, \ 14, \ 15\}$$

EXERCISE 3-11

Define an average function **means(C)** which returns the geometric mean, the quadratic mean and the harmonic mean of a set of elements C. As an application, find the geometric, harmonic and quadratic means of the sets {1,5,6,7,9} and {a, b, c, d, e, f, g, h}.

To define *means(C)*, we create the following procedure:

```
>> maple('means:=proc(C::set) local g,c,h,i,j,k; g:=(mul(i,i=C)^(1/nops(C)));
c:=sqrt(add(j^2,j=C)/nops(C));h:=nops(C)/add(1/k,k=C); 'geomean='.g,
'quadmean=' .c, 'harmean=' .h;end;')'))
```

Now we can calculate the quadratic, geometric and harmonic means of the proposed sets.

```
>> pretty(sym(maple('means({1,5,6,7,9}) ')))
```

$$geomean =.(1890)^{1/5}, \quad quadmean =.(8/5 \ 15)^{1/2}, \quad harmean =. \ \frac{3150}{1021}$$

```
>> pretty (sym (maple ('means({a,b,c,d,e,f,g,h})')))
```

$$geomean =.((g \ c \ h \ b \ e \ f \ a \ d))^{1/8}, quadmean =.$$

$$(1/4 \ (2 \ g^2 + 2 \ c^2 + 2 \ h^2 + 2 \ b^2 + 2 \ e^2 + 2 \ f^2 + 2 \ a^2 + 2 \ d^2)^{1/2} \ ),$$

$$harmean =. \ \frac{8}{1/g + 1/c + 1/h + 1/b + 1/e + 1/f + 1/a + 1/d}$$

CHAPTER 4

■ ■ ■

Vector Spaces and Linear Applications. Equations and Systems

4.1 Matrix Algebra and Vector Spaces

Matrix algebra has a strong field of application in the theory of vector spaces, particularly in the study of types of linear transformations between vector spaces, linear forms, bilinear forms, quadratic forms, etc. It is also plays a critical role in the study of systems of linear equations.

The following MATLAB commands are useful when working in the above mentioned fields:

nullspace (A) returns a basis for the kernel of *A*.

N = null (A) generates an orthonormal basis for the kernel of *A*. The number of columns of *N* is the dimension of the kernel (the nullity) of *A*.

Q = orth (A) generates an orthonormal basis for the range of *A*, i.e., the columns of *Q* generate the same space as the columns of *A*, and the number of columns in *Q* is the rank of *A*.

colspace(A) returns a basis for the columns of *A*.

dot (A, B) gives the dot product of vectors *A* and *B*.

cross (A, B) gives the vector product of vectors *A* and *B*.

subspace (A, B) finds the angle between two subspaces specified by the columns of A and B. If A and B are column vectors of unit length, this is the same as acos(abs(A'*B)).

maple ('kernel(A)') or maple ('nullspace (A)') returns a basis for the kernel of *A*.

maple ('nullspace(A,n)') or maple ('kernel(A,n)') returns a basis for the kernel of *A* and assigns to *n* the dimension of the kernel.

maple ('colspace(A)') returns a basis for the columns of *A*.

maple ('colspace(A,n)') returns a basis for the columns of *A* and assigns to *n* the dimension of the column space.

maple ('colspan(A)') returns the generator set of vectors for the column space of the matrix *A*, whose elements can be multivariate polynomials over the rational numbers.

maple ('colspan(A,n)') returns the generator set of vectors for the column space of the matrix A and assigns to n the dimension of the column space.

maple ('rowspace(A)') returns a basis for the rows of the matrix A.

maple ('rowspace(A,n)') returns a basis for the rows of A and assigns to n the dimension of the row space.

maple ('rowspan(A)') returns a generator set of vectors for the row space of the matrix A, whose elements can be multivariate polynomials over the rational numbers.

maple ('rowspan(A,n)') returns the generator set of vectors for the row space of the matrix A, and assigns to n the dimension of the row space.

maple ('dotprod(A, B)') gives the dot product of vectors A and B.

maple ('dotprod(A,B,'orthogonal')') gives the dot product of vectors A and B in an orthogonal space.

maple ('crossprod(A, B)') gives the vector product of vectors A and B.

maple ('innerprod (V1 A V2)') computes the inner product of the vectors $V1$ and $V2$ and the matrix A.

maple('innerprod(V1,A1,...,An,V2)') calculates the inner product of the vectors $V1$ and $V2$ and the matrices $A1, A2,..., An$.

maple ('angle(A, B)') gives the angle formed by the vectors A and B.

maple ('norm (V)') returns the infinity norm of the vector V (the maximum of its elements).

maple ('norm(V, option)') returns the norm of the vector V where the type of norm is specified by the option. Possible options are 'infinity', 'frobenius' or any positive integer. The Frobenius norm is the square root of the sum of squares of the components, the k-norm (positive integer k) is the kth root of the sum of the kth powers of the components.

maple ('normalize (V)') normalizes the vector V (using the 2-norm of V).

maple ('basis({v1,v2,...,vn})') gives a basis of the vector space generated by the set of vectors $\{v1, v2,..., vn\}$.

maple ('sumbasis({Vs1},{Vs2},...,{Vsn})') gives a basis for the sum of the vector spaces generated by the sets of vectors $\{Vs1\}, \{Vs2\},..., \{Vsn\}$.

maple('intbasis({Vs1},{Vs2},...,{Vsn})') gives a basis for the intersection of the vector spaces generated by the sets of vectors $\{Vs1\}, \{Vs2\},..., \{Vsn\}$.

maple('GramSchmidt({v1,v2,...,vn})') uses the Gram–Schmidt process to create an orthogonal basis from the set of vectors $\{v1,v2,...,vn\}$. The basis does not have to be orthonormal.

4.2 Linear Independence, Bases, and Base Change

EXERCISE 4-1

Determine which of the following sets of vectors are linearly independent:

$$\{\{2,3,-1\}, \{0,0,1\}, \{2,1,0\}\}$$

$$\{\{1,2,-3,4\},\{3,-1,2,1\},\{1,-5,8,-7\},\{2,3,1,-1\}\}$$

$$\{\{1,2,2,1\},\{3,4,4,3\},\{1,0,0,1\}\}$$

```
>> A = [2,3,-1; 0,0,1; 2,1,0]

A =

2   3   -1
0   0    1
2   1    0

>> det(A)

ans =

4
```

Since the determinant is non-zero, the vectors are linearly independent.

```
>> B = [1,2,-3,4;3,-1,2,1;1,-5,8,-7;2,3,1,-1]

B =

1    2   -3  4
3   -1    2  1
1   -5    8 -7
2    3    1 -1

>> det(B)

ans =

0
```

Since the determinant is zero, the vectors are linearly dependent:

```
>> C = [1,2,2,1;3,4,4,3;1,0,0,1]

C =

1     2     2     1
3     4     4     3
1     0     0     1
```

```
>> rank(C)
```

ans =

2

As we have only three vectors in a space of dimension four, we cannot apply the determinant test, but they will be linearly independent if the rank of the corresponding matrix is 3. Since we see that the rank is 2, the vectors are linearly dependent.

EXERCISE 4-2

Find the dimension and a basis of the space generated by the following set of vectors:

$$\{\{2,3,4,-1,1\},\{3,4,7,-2,-1\},\{1,3,-1,1,8\},\{0,5,5,-1,4\}\}$$

The dimension of the space generated by a set of vectors is equal to the rank of the matrix formed by the vectors:

```
>> A = [2,3,4,-1,1;3,4,7,-2,-1;1,3,-1,1,8;0,5,5,-1,4]
```

A =

2	3	4	-1	1
3	4	7	-2	-1
1	3	-1	1	8
0	5	5	-1	4

```
>> rank(A)
```

ans =

3

The rank of the array is 3, so the requested dimension is 3.

To find a basis, we considered any non-singular matrix minor of order 3. The vectors containing components included in this minor will form a basis.

```
>> det([2,3,4;3,4,7;0,5,5])
```

ans =

-15

Then, a basis of the generated linear space is the set of vectors *{{2,3,4,−1,1},{3,4,7,−2,−1},{0,5,5,−1,4}}*.

A basis can be calculated directly in the following way:

```
>> pretty(sym(maple('basis({vector([2,3,4,-1,1]),vector([3,4,7,-2,-1]),
   (((vector([1,3,-1,1,8]), vector ([0,5,5,-1,4])})')))
```

```
[2    3    4    -1    1]
[                      ]
[3    4    7    -2    -1]
[                      ]
[0    5    5    -1    4]
```

EXERCISE 4-3

Determine whether the set of vectors

$$\{\{2,3,-1\}, \{0,0,1\}, \{2,1,0\}\}$$

forms a basis of R^3, and if so, find the components of the vector $x = (3,5,1)$ with respect to this basis.

```
>> det([2,3,-1;0,0,1;2,1,0])
```

ans =

4

Since we have three vectors in a space of dimension 3, they will form a basis if the determinant of the corresponding matrix is non-zero. Thus, we see that they do indeed form a basis.

The components of the vector (3,5,1) with respect to this basis are found as follows:

```
>> inv([2,0,2;3,0,1;-1,1,0]) * [3,5,1]'
```

ans =

1.7500
2.7500
-0.2500

EXERCISE 4-4

Consider the bases B and $B1$ of three-dimensional real vector space R^3:

$$B = \{\{1,0,0\}, \{-1, 1, 0\}, \{0,1,-1\}\}$$

$$B1 = \{\{1,0,-1\}, \{2,1,0\}, \{-1, 1, 1\}\}$$

Find the matrix for the change of basis B to $B1$ and calculate the components of the vector $\{2,1,3\}$ in base B with respect to the basis $B1$.

```
>> B = [1,0,0;-1,1,0;0,1,-1];
```

```
>> B1 = [1,0,-1;2,1,0;-1,1,1];
```

```
>> A = inv(B1')*B'
```

A =

```
-0.5000   1.5000   2.5000
 0.5000  -0.5000  -0.5000
-0.5000   1.5000   1.5000
```

```
>> sym (A)
```

ans =

```
[-1/2,   3/2,   5/2]
[ 1/2,  -1/2,  -1/2]
[-1/2,   3/2,   3/2]
```

We already have the change of basis matrix. Now we find the components of the B-vector [2,3,1] with respect to the basis B1.

```
>> sym(inv(B1')*B'*[2,1,3]')
```

ans =

```
[8]
[-1]
[5]
```

EXERCISE 4-5

Let *V* be a vector space of dimension 5 with basis $B = \{u1,\ldots, u5\}$. Let L be the space generated by the vectors $a1 = u1 - u2 + 3u3 + 2u4 + 5u5$, $a2 = u1 + u2 + u3 + 2u4 + 3u5$, $a3 = u1 + u3 - u4 + 2u5$. Let *M* be the space generated by $b1 = 13u1 + 2u2 + 3u3 + 8u4 + 8u5$ and $b2 = 17u1 + 3u2 + 3u3 + 10u4 + 9u5$. Find a basis for *L+M* and another for *L∩M*.

The linear space *L* is generated by the vectors with components [1,–1, 3, 2, 5], [1,1,1,2,3] and [1,0,1,–1,2] with respect to the basis *B*. The space *M* is generated by the vectors with components [13,2,3,8,8] and [17,3,3,10,9] with respect to the basis *B*. We find a basis for *L+M* in the following way:

```
>> pretty(sym(maple('sumbasis({vector([1,-1,3,2,5]), vector([1,1,1,2,3]),
   (((vector([1,0,1,-1,2])}, {vector([13,2,3,8,8]), vector([17,3,3,10,9])})')))
```

ans =

```
[17, 1, 1, 13]
[3,  0, 1,  2]
[3,  1, 1,  3]
[10 -1, 2,  8]
[9,  2, 3,  8]
```

Therefore the dimension of *L+M* is 4.

The above matrix columns form a basis of $L+M$. Now we calculate a basis for $L \cap M$ as follows:

```
>> pretty(sym(maple('intbasis({vector([1,-1,3,2,5]), vector([1,1,1,2,3]),
   (((vector([1,0,1,-1,2])}, {vector([13,2,3,8,8]), vector([17,3,3,10,9])})')))
```

ans =

```
[-1]
[1]
[-3]
[-2]
[-5]
```

Therefore the dimension of $L \cap M$ is 4.

4.3 Vector Geometry in 2 and 3 Dimensions

EXERCISE 4-6

Normalize the vectors $x1 = (1,1,-1)$ and $x2 = (1, 1, 1)$, determine if they are orthogonal and find their vector product.

```
>> pretty(sym(maple('normalize(vector([1,1,-1]))')))
```

$$[1/3 \ 3^{1/2} \quad 1/3 \ 3^{1/2} \quad - 1/3 \ 3^{1/2} \ ]$$

```
>> pretty(sym(maple('normalize(vector([1,1,1]))')))
```

$$[1/3 \ 3^{1/2} \quad 1/3 \ 3^{1/2} \quad 1/3 \ 3^{1/2} \ ]$$

The vectors are orthogonal if their scalar product is zero:

```
>> dot([1,1,-1],[1,1,1])
```

ans =

1

Thus, the vectors are orthogonal. We now calculate their vector product:

```
>> cross([1,1,-1],[1,1,1])
```

ans =

2 - 2 0

Thus, the vector product is the vector $(2,-2, 0)$.

EXERCISE 4-7

Find the vector triple product of the vectors (1,1,2), (0,1,0), (0,1,1).

```
>> dot([1,1,2], cross ([0,1,0], [0,1,1]))
```

ans = 1

EXERCISE 4-8

Using the Gram-Schmidt process, find an orthogonal basis from the vectors (1,0,0), (1,1,0), (0,1,1).

```
>> maple('GramSchmidt ([vector([1,0,0]), vector([1,1,0]), vector([0,1,1])])')
```

ans =

[[1, 0, 0], [0, 1, 0], [0, 0, 1]]

EXERCISE 4-9

Find the area of the triangle whose vertices are at (0,0), (5,1) and (3,7).

```
>> (1/2) * det([0,0,1;5,1,1;3,7,1])
```

ans =

16

Here we have applied a well-known formula for the area of a triangle based on the coordinates of its vertices.

EXERCISE 4-10

Find the angle formed by the vectors $a = (1,2,3)$ and $b = (0,3,1)$.

```
>> pretty(sym(maple('angle([1,2,3],[0,3,1])')))
```

$$acos(9/140 \ 14^{1/2} \ 10^{1/2})$$

Now, we approximate the result:

>> **vpa(ans)**

ans =

.7064997155064410

4.4 Linear Applications

EXERCISE 4-11

Given the linear transformation whose matrix is given by the set of vectors

{(0,–3,–1,–3,–1),(–3,3,–3,–3,–1),(2,2,–1,1,2)}

find a basis for its kernel. Also find the image of the vectors (4,2,0,0,–6) and (1,2, –1,–2, 3) under this linear transformation.

>> **A = [0,-3,-1,-3,-1;-3,3,-3,-3,-1;2,2,-1,1,2]**

A =

```
   0    -3    -1    -3    -1
  -3     3    -3    -3    -1
   2     2    -1     1     2
```

>> **null(A)**

ans =

```
-0.5540   0
-0.3380   0.2236
-0.1828   0.6708
 0.1584  -0.5814
 0.7213   0.4025
```

The two columns of the previous output form a basis of the kernel of T, so the dimension of the kernel will be 2:

>> **maple('T:=x->multiply(array([[0,-3,-1,-3,-1],[-3,3,-3,-3,-1],[2,2,-1,1,2]]),x)')**
>> **pretty(sym(maple('T([4,2,0,0,-6])')))**

$$[0 \quad 0 \quad 0]$$

>> **pretty(sym(maple('T([1,2,-1,-2,3])')))**

$$[- 2 \quad 9 \quad 11]$$

EXERCISE 4-12

We consider the linear transformation f between two vector subspaces U and V such that $f(e1) = v1\text{-}v2$, $f(e2) = v2\text{-}v3$ and $f(e3) = v3\text{-}v4$, where:

$$B = \{e1, e2, e3\} \text{ is a basis of } U \text{ (a subspace of } R^3)$$

$$B' = \{v1, v2, v3, v4\} \text{ is a basis of } V \text{ (a subspace of } R^4)$$

Find the matrix associated with the transformation f. Find the image of the vector $v=(1,1,2)$ of U under the linear transformation f.

The matrix associated with f is evident, we need only examine the definition of f.

```
>> A = [1,0,0;-1,1,0;0,-1,1;0,0,1]
```

A =

```
 1     0     0
-1     1     0
 0    -1     1
 0     0     1
```

```
>> maple('T1:=x->multiply(array([[1,0,0],[-1,1,0],[0,-1,1],[0,0,1]]),x)');
>> pretty(sym(maple('T1([1,1,2])')))
```

$$[1\ 0\ 1\ 2]$$

EXERCISE 4-13

Consider the linear transformation f between two vector subspaces U and V of three-dimensional real space, so that $f(a,b,c) = (a+b,b+c,a+c)$, for (a, b, c) in U.

Find the matrix associated to the transformations f, f^5 and e^f

```
>> maple('T:=(a,b,c)->[a+b,b+c,a+c]');
```

To find the matrix of f, we will consider the image of the canonical basis vectors under the transformation f:

```
>> [maple('T(1,0,0)'), maple('T(0,1,0)'),maple('T(0,0,1)')]
```

ans =

```
[1, 0, 1] [1, 1, 0] [0, 1, 1]
```

The matrix whose columns are the above vectors is the matrix of the linear transformation f, which can be found directly via:

```
>> A = sym(maple('transpose(array([T(1,0,0),T(0,1,0),T(0,0,1)]))'))
```

A =

```
[1, 1, 0]
[0, 1, 1]
[1, 0, 1]
```

The matrix associated to f^5 will be given by A^5:

```
>> A ^ 5
```

ans =

```
11 10 11
11 11 10
10 11 11
```

The matrix associated to e^f will be e^A:

```
>> expm(A)
```

ans =

```
3.1751       2.8321          1.3819
1.3819       3.1751          2.8321
2.8321       1.3819          3.1751
```

EXERCISE 4-14

Consider the linear transformation f between two vector subspaces U (contained in R^3) and V (contained in R^4), so that $f(a,b,c) = (a,0,c,0)$ for all (a, b, c) in U.

Find the matrix associated to the transformation f, its kernel and the dimensions of the kernel and the image of f.

```
>> maple('T:=(a,b,c)->[a,0,c,0]');
>> A = sym(maple('transpose(array([T(1,0,0),T(0,1,0),T(0,0,1)]))'))
```

A =

```
[1, 0, 0]
[0, 0, 0]
[0, 0, 1]
[0, 0, 0]
```

125

The kernel is the set of vectors of U with null image in V:

```
>> null(A)
```

ans =

[0]
[1]
[0]

Thus the kernel will be the set of vectors $(0,b,0)$, for b varying in U. In addition, the kernel obviously has dimension 1, since we have shown that a basis is given by the single vector (0,1,0):

```
>> maple('rank(matrix(4,3,[1,0,0,0,0,0,0,0,1,0,0,0]))')
```

ans =

2

The dimension of the image of f is 2, since the sum of the dimensions of the kernel and the image must be the dimension of U (which is 3). On the other hand, the dimension of the image of f must match the rank of the matrix of the linear transformation, which is 2. Two column vectors containing the elements of a non-singular minor of the matrix of f will form a basis of the image of f:

```
>> det([1,0;0,1])
```

ans =

1

Thus, a basis of the image of f will be {(1,0,0,0),(0,0,1,0)}.

EXERCISE 4-15

Consider the bilinear form $f: U \times V \to R$, where U and V are two vector subspaces of three-dimensional real space R^3, such that:

$$f[\{(x1, x2, x3), (y1, y2, y3)\}] = x1\ y1 - 2x1\ y2 + 4x2\ y3 - x3\ y1 - 3\ x3\ y3$$

Find the matrix associated with the bilinear form f and classify it.

```
>> maple('A:=array([[1,-2,0],[0,0,4],[-1,0,-3]])');pretty(sym(maple('A')))
```

```
[ 1    -2    0]
[             ]
[ 0     0    4]
[             ]
[-1     0   -3]
```

```
>> pretty(expand (sym (maple ('evalm ([[x 1, x 2, x 3]] & * A & * transpose([[y1, y2, y3]]))'))));)
```

$$y1\ x1 - y1\ x3 - 2\ x1\ y2 + 4\ y3\ x2 - 3\ x3\ y3$$

Then, the f matrix is $\{\{1, -2, 0\}, \{0,0,4\}, \{-1, 0, -3\}\}$.

```
maple('det (A)');
```

8

As the determinant of the matrix of f is non-zero, the bilinear form is regular non-degenerate.

4.5 Quadratic Forms

EXERCISE 4-16

Consider the quadratic form $f: U \rightarrow R$, where U is a vector subspace of real three-dimensional space R^3, such that:

$$f[(x,y,z)] = x^2 - 2xy + y^2 + 6xz - 3yz + 4z^2$$

Find the matrix associated with f and classify it.

```
>>  maple('A:=array([[1,-1,3],[-1,1,-3/2],[3,-3/2,4]])');pretty(sym(maple('A')));
```

```
[ 1      -1      3  ]
[                   ]
[-1       1     -3/2]
[                   ]
[ 3     -3/2     4  ]
```

```
>> pretty(simplify(sym(maple('evalm([[x, y, z]] & * A & * transpose ([[x, y, z]]))'))))
```

$$x^2 - 2 x y + 6 x z + y^2 - 3 y z + 4 z^2$$

Thus, A is the matrix associated with f.

To classify it, we find the corresponding determinants.

```
>> pretty(sym(maple('det(A)')));
```

-9/4

```
>> pretty(sym(maple('det([[1,-1],[-1,1]])')));
```

0

The quadratic form is negative semidefinite.

However, we can also obtain the classification via the eigenvalues of the matrix of the quadratic form.

A quadratic form is defined to be positive definite if and only if all its eigenvalues are strictly positive. A quadratic form is defined to be negative definite if and only if all its eigenvalues are strictly negative.

A quadratic form is positive semidefinite if and only if all its eigenvalues are non-negative. A quadratic form is negative semidefinite if and only if all its eigenvalues are not positive.

A quadratic form is indefinite if it has both positive and negative eigenvalues.

>> **pretty(sym(maple('evalf(eigenvals(A))')))**

$$6.4498046649069250305217677941300 +.2 \ 10^{-31} \ i,$$

$$-.85690615612023945647201856979180 -.1 \ 10^{-31} \ i,$$

$$.40710149121331442595025077566180 -.1 \ 10^{-31} \ i$$

All of the eigenvalues are complex, so the quadratic form is indefinite.

EXERCISE 4-17

Consider the quadratic form $f: U \rightarrow R$, where U is a vector subspace of real three-dimensional space R^3, such that:

$$f[(x, y, z)] = x^2 + 2y^2 + 4yz + 2z^2$$

Find the matrix associated with f and classify it. Find its reduced form, its rank and its signature.

>> **maple('A:=array([[1,0,0],[0,2,2],[0,2,2]])');pretty(sym(maple('A')))**

```
[1 0 0]
[     ]
[0 2 2]
[     ]
[0 2 2]
```

>> **pretty(simplify(sym(maple('evalm([[x, y, z]] & * A & * transpose ([[x, y, z]]))'))))**

$$x^2 + 2 \ y^2 + 4 \ y \ z + 2 \ z^2$$

Thus, the matrix of the quadratic form is the matrix A.

>> **pretty(sym(maple('det(A)')))**

0

>> **pretty(sym(maple('det([[1,0],[0,2]])')))**

2

The quadratic form is degenerate positive semidefinite.

To find the reduced form, we diagonalize the matrix:

```
>> pretty(sym(maple('jordan(A)')))
```

```
[0 0 0]
[     ]
[0 1 0]
[     ]
[0 0 4]
```

```
>> pretty(sym(maple('evalm([[a, b, c]] & * jordan (A) & * transpose ([[a, b, c]]))')))
```

$$a^2 + 4c^2$$

Thus, the reduced form is given by $f(a,b,c) = a^2 + 4c^2$.

```
>> pretty(sym(maple('rank(jordan(matrix(3,3,[1,0,0,0,2,2,0,2,2])))')))
```

2

The rank of the quadratic form is 2, since the rank of the matrix is 2. The signature is also 2, since the number of positive terms in the diagonal of the diagonal matrix is 2.

4.6 Equations and Systems

MATLAB offers certain commands that allow you to solve equations and systems. Among them are the following:

solve('equation', 'x') solves the equation with respect to the variable x.

syms x; solve(equ(x), x) solves the equation *equ(x)* with respect to the variable x.

solve('eq1,eq2,...,eqn', 'x1,x2,...,xn') solves the simultaneous equations *eq1,...,eqn* (in terms of the system variables $x1,..., xn$).

syms x1 x2 ... xn ; solve(eq1, eq2, ..., eqn, x1, x2, ..., xn) solves the simultaneous equations *eq1,...,eqn* (in terms of the system variables $x1,..., xn$).

X = linsolve(A,B) solves $A * X = B$ for a square matrix A, and matrices B and X.

x = nnls (A, b) solves $A * X = b$ using the method of least squares, where x is a vector $(x \geq 0)$.

x = lscov(A,b,V) gives the vector X that minimizes $(A * x - b)' * inv (V) * (A * x - b)$.

roots(V) gives the roots of the polynomial whose coefficients are the components of the vector V.

X = A\B solves the system $A * X = B$.

X = A/B solves the system $X * A = B$.

In addition, equations and systems of equations can be solved using the following commands (all of them must be preceded by the *maple* command):

solve(equation, variable) solves the given equation for the given variable.

solve (expression, variable) solves the equation *expression = 0* for the given variable.

solve({expr1,..,exprn},{var1,..,varn}) solves the given system of equations for the specified variables.

solve(equation) solves the equation for all of its variables.

solve(expr1,...,exprn) solves the system specified by the equations for all possible variables.

solve(inequal, variable) solves the inequality for the specified variable.

solve(s, var) solves the equation in the series *s* for the specified variable.

subs(solutions, equations) substitutes the given list of solutions into the equations, to verify solutions.

lhs (equation) returns the left-hand side of the equation.

lhs (inequality) returns the left-hand side of the inequality.

rhs (equation) returns the right-hand side of the equation.

rhs (inequality) returns the right-hand side of the inequality.

readlib (isolate): isolate (equation, expression) isolates the expression in the equation and attemtps to solve for it.

readlib (isolate): isolate (expr1, expr2) equivalent to isolate (expr1=0, expr2).

reablib (isolate): isolate (equation, expression, n) The integer *n* controls the maximum number of transformation steps that isolate performs. The default is 100000.

testeq(expr1=expr2) or testeq (expr1, expr2) tests if the expressions are equivalent. The purpose may be to eliminate redundant equations in a system.

eliminate (setequ, setvar) eliminates the given set of variables in the set of specified equations.

isolve (equation) gives the integer solutions of the given equation for all of its variables.

isolve (expression) gives the integer solutions of the equation expression = 0 for all of its variables.

isolve({equ1,..,equn}) gives the integer solutions to the specified system of equations for all variables.

isolve (equation, variable) gives the integer solutions of the specified equation in the given variable.

isolve({equ1,...,equn},{var1,...,varn}) gives the integer solutions of the specified system in the given variables.

isolve(equation,{var1,...,varn}) gives the integer solutions of the specified equation in the given variables.

fsolve (equation, variable) solves the given equation using Newton's method.

fsolve (expression, variable) solves the equation *expression = 0* in the given variable using Newton's method.

fsolve ({equ1,...,equn},{var1,...,varn}) solves the system of equations for the given variables using numerical methods (the number of equations equals the number of unknowns).

fsolve (expr) or fsolve({equ1,...,equn}) solves the equation *expr = 0* for the system using numerical methods.

fsolve (equation,var,a..b) solves the equation in the variable *var* by numerical methods, obtaining solutions in the interval [a, b].

fsolve ({equ1,...,equn},{var1,...,varn},{var1=a1..b1,..., varn = an...bn}) finds real solutions of the system in the given variables that are in the specified intervals (by numerical methods).

fsolve (equation, variable, complex) finds the complex solutions of the given equation.

fsolve (equation,variable,'maxsols'=m) finds up to m solutions of the given equation.

fsolve (equation, variable, 'fulldigits') ensures an optimum value of Digits in order to compute the largest number of possible solutions of the given equation in the specified variable.

msolve(equation, m) solves the equation modulo m in all its variables.

msolve(expression, m) solves the equation expression = 0 modulo m in all its variables.

msolve({equ1,...,equn},m) solves the given system modulo m in all its variables.

msolve(equation,variable,m) or msolve(equation,{var1,...,varn},m) solves the equation modulo *m* in the variable or variables specified.

msolve({equ1,...,equn},{var1,...,varn},m) solves the given system modulo *m* in the specified variables.

RootOf (equation, variable) represents the roots of the given equation in the specified variable in the form of RootOf expressions. For certain equations it is only possible to express the solutions in terms of RootOf expressions.

RootOf (expression, variable) presents the solutions of the equation *expression = 0* in terms of RootOf expressions.

RootOf (equation) presents the solutions of the given univariate equation in terms of RootOf expressions.

allvalues (expr) Expressions involving RootOfs often evaluate to more than one value or expression. The allvalues command returns all possible values. It uses solve to calculate the exact roots of the expression, and if this is impossible, it uses fsolve to calculate the approximate solutions.

allvalues(expr,d) indicates that identical RootOfs in the expression are only to be evaluated once, thus avoiding redundancy and reducing the calculation time.

convert (ineq, equality) converts the given inequality to an equation by replacing the symbols < or < = by =.

convert (equ, lessequal) converts the given equation or strict inequality to a non-strict inequality replacing the symbols < or = by < =.

convert (equ, lessthan) converts the given equation or non-strict inequality to the corresponding strict inequality replacing the symbols = or < = by the symbol <.

with(student):equate(list1,list2) creates a set of equations of the form *{list1[1] = list2[1],..., list1[n] = list2[n]}*.

equate(list) creates a set of equations of the form *{list [1] = 0,..., list [n] = 0}*.

equate (array1, array2) converts the two arrays to a set of equations.

equate (table1, table2) converts the two tables to a set of equations.

equate (expr1, expr2) converts the two expressions to the set containing the equation *expr1 = expr2.*

Here are some examples:

First, we solve an equation in exact and approximate form and check one of the solutions.

```
>> pretty(sym(maple('eq := x^4-5*x^2+6*x=2: solve(eq,x)')))
```

$$-1 + 3^{1/2} , -1 - 3^{1/2} , 1, 1$$

```
>> pretty(sym(maple('sols := [solve(eq,x)] : evalf(sols,10)')))
```

$$[.732050808 \quad -2.732050808 \quad 1. \quad 1.]$$

```
>> pretty(simple(sym(maple('subs( x=sols[1], eq )'))))
```

$$2 = 2$$

The above equation also can be solved as follows:

```
>> solve('x^4-5*x^2+6*x=2')
```

ans =

```
[- 1 + 3 ^(1/2)]
[- 1 - 3 ^(1/2)]
[            1]
[            1]
```

Another way to solve the same equation would be as follows:

```
>> syms x
>> solve(x^4-5*x^2+6*x-2)
```

ans =

```
[- 1 + 3 ^(1/2)]
[- 1 - 3 ^(1/2)]
[            1]
[            1]
```

Next we solve a system of equations and check their solutions.

```
>>  maple('eqns:= {u+v+w=1, 3*u+v=3, u-2*v-w=0}:sols:= solve(eqns)')
```

ans =

sols: = {w = -2/5, v = 3/5, u = 4/5}

```
>> maple('subs( sols, eqns )')
```

ans =

{1 = 1, 0 = 0, 3 = 3}

The previous system also can be solved in the following way:

```
>> syms u v w
>> [u, v, w] = solve(u+v+w-1, 3*u+v-3, u-2*v-w, u,v,w)
```

u =

4/5

v =

3/5

w =

-2/5

Alternatively, we can solve the system as follows:

```
>> [u, v, w] = solve('u+v+w=1', '3*u+v=3', 'u-2*v-w=0', 'u','v','w')
```

u =

4/5

v =

3/5

w =

-2/5

Or we can do the following:

```
>> [u, v, w] = solve('u+v+w=1, 3*u+v=3, u-2*v-w=0', 'u,v,w')
```

u =

4/5

v =

3/5

w =

-2/5

Next we solve some systems subject to certain conditions.

```
>> pretty(sym(maple('solve({x^2*y^2=0, x-y=1})')))
```

$$\{x = 0, \ y = -1\}, \ \{x = 0, \ y = -1\}, \ \{x = 1, \ y = 0\}, \ \{x = 1, \ y = 0\}$$

```
>> pretty(sym(maple('solve({x^2*y^2=0, x-y=1, x<>0}) ')))
```

$$\{x = 1, \ y = 0\}, \ \{x = 1, \ y = 0\}$$

```
>> pretty(sym(maple('solve({x^2*y^2-b, x^2-y^2-a}, {x,y}) ')))
```

$$\{y = 1/2 \ \%4, \ x = 1/2 \ \%3\}, \ \{y = 1/2 \ \%4, \ x = -1/2 \ \%3\},$$

$$\{y = -1/2 \ \%4, \ x = 1/2 \ \%3\}, \ \{y = -1/2 \ \%4, \ x = -1/2 \ \%3\},$$

$$\{y = 1/2 \ \%1, \ x = 1/2 \ \%2\}, \ \{x = -1/2 \ \%2, \ y = 1/2 \ \%1\},$$

$$\{y = -1/2 \ \%1, \ x = 1/2 \ \%2\}, \ \{x = -1/2 \ \%2, \ y = -1/2 \ \%1\}\}$$

$$\%1: \ = (-2 \ a - 2 \ (a + 4 \ (b)^2)^{1/2})^{1/2}$$

$$\%2: \ = (2 \ a - 2 \ (a + 4 \ (b)^2)^{1/2})^{1/2}$$

$$3\%: \ = (2 + 2 \ (a + 4 \ (b)^2)^{1/2})^{1/2}$$

$$\%4: \ = (-2 \ a + 2 \ (a + 4 \ (b)^2)^{1/2})^{1/2}$$

Now we find the integer solutions of an equation.

```
>> pretty(sym(maple('isolve(3*x-4*y=7) ')))
```

$$\{y = 2 + 3 \ \_N1, \ x = 5 + 4 \ \_N1\}$$

We solve a system and an equation approximately.

```
>> maple('f: = sin(x + y) - exp(x) * y = 0: ' g: = x ^ 2 - y = 2: ');
>> pretty(sym(maple('fsolve({f,g},{x,y},{x=-1..1,y=-2..0}) ')))
```

$$\{y = -1.552838698, \ x = -.6687012050\}$$

```
>> maple('f: = 10-(ln(v+(v^2-1)^(1/2))-ln(3+(3^2-1)^(1/2)))') ;

>> pretty(sym(maple('fsolve(f,v)')))
```

$$64189.82535$$

```
>> pretty(sym(maple('fsolve(f,v,1..infinity)')))
```

$$64189.82535$$

In the two following equations, instead of isolating x, we isolate $sin (x)$ in the first equation and x^2 in the second equation.

```
>> pretty(sym(maple('readlib(isolate):isolate(4*x*sin(x)=3,sin(x))')))
```

$$sin \ (x) = 3/4 \ x$$

```
>> pretty(sym(maple('isolate(x^2-3*x-5,x^2) ')))
```

$$x^2 = 3 \ x + 5$$

We now verify that two expressions are not equal, but are probabilistically equivalent.

```
>> maple('a: = (sin (x) ^ 2 - cos (x) * tan (x)) * (sin (x) ^ 2 + cos (x) * tan (x)) ^ 2:)
   b: = 1/4 * sin(2*x) ^ 2 - 1/2 * sin(2*x) * cos (x) - 2 * cos (x) ^ 2
        + 1/2 * sin(2*x) * cos (x) ^ 3 + 3 * cos (x) ^ 4 - cos (x) ^ 6:');

>> pretty(sym(maple('evalb( a = b ) ')))
```

$$false$$

```
>> pretty(sym(maple('evalb( expand(a) = expand(b) )')))
```

$$false$$

```
>> pretty(sym(maple('testeq( a = b )')))
```

$$true$$

In the following example, we eliminate a variable from a system:

```
>> pretty(sym(maple('readlib(eliminate): eliminate({x ^ 2 + y ^ 2-1, x ^ 3 - y ^ 2 * x + x * y-3}, x)')))
```

$$\left[\{x = - \frac{3}{2 \ y^2 - y - 1}\}, \ \{4 \ y^6 - 7 \ y^4 - 4 \ y^5 + 6 \ y^3 + 4 \ y^2 - 2 \ y + 8\}\right]$$

EXERCISE 4-18

Find the solutions to the following equations:

$\sin(x)\cos(x) = 0$, $\sin(x) = a\cos(x)$, $ax \wedge 2 + bx + c = 0$ and $\sin(x) + \cos(x) = \text{sqrt}(3)/2$.

```
>> solve('sin(x) * cos(x) = 0')
```

ans =

```
[        0]
[1/2 * pi]
[-1/2 * pi]
```

```
>> solve('sin(x) = a * cos(x) ',' x')
```

ans =

atan (a)

```
>> solve('a*x^2+b*x+c=0','x')
```

ans =

```
[1/2/a * (-b + (b ^ 2-4 * a * c) ^(1/2))]
[1/2/a * (-b-(b^2-4*a*c) ^(1/2))]
```

```
>> solve('sin(x)+cos(x)=sqrt(3)/2')
```

ans =

```
[1/2 * 3 ^(1/2)]
[1/2 * 3 ^(1/2)]
```

EXERCISE 4-19

Find at least two solutions of each of the following two trigonometric and exponential equations:

$$x\sin(x) = \frac{1}{2} \quad \text{and} \quad 2^{x^3} = 4(2^{3x}).$$

First, we use the command *fsolve*:

```
>> maple('fsolve(x * sin (x) = 1/2)')
```

ans =

-.74084095509549062101093540994313

```
>> maple('fsolve(2^(x^3)=4*2^(3*x))')
```

ans =

2.00000000000000000000000000000000

For both equations we get a single solution. To find more solutions, we graph the functions to find approximate intervals where possible solutions might fall. See Figure 4-1:

```
>> fplot('[x * sin(x) - 1/2.0]', [0, 4 * pi])
```

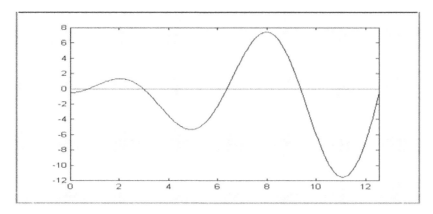

Figure 4-1.

We observe that there is a solution between 0 and 2, another between 2 and 4, another between 4 and 8, and so on. We can calculate three of them:

```
((' s1=maple('fsolve(x*sin(x)=1/2,x,0..2)')
```

s1 =

.7408409550954906

```
>> s2=maple('fsolve(x*sin(x)=1/2,x,2..4)')
```

s2 =

2.972585490382360

```
>> s3=maple('fsolve(x*sin(x)=1/2,x,4..8)')
```

S3 =

6.361859813361645

We repeat this process for the second equation, starting with the graph (see Figure 4-2):

```
>> subplot(2,1,1)
>> fplot('[2^(x^3),4*2^(3*x)]',[-3,1,-1/4,3/2])
>> subplot(2,1,2)
>> fplot('[2^(x^3),4*2^(3*x)]',[1,3,100,400])
```

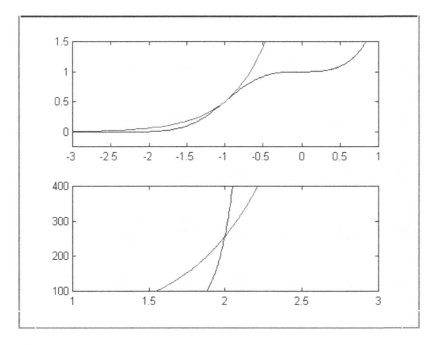

Figure 4-2.

Two parts of the graph are shown where there are intersections. There are possible solutions between −4 and 0, and between 0 and 3. Given this information we try to calculate these solutions:

```
>> maple('fsolve(2 ^(x^3) = 4 * 2 ^(3*x), x, - 4.. 0)')
```

ans =

-1.00000000000

```
>> maple('fsolve(2^(x^3)=4*2^(3*x),x,0..3)')
```

ans =

2.00000000000

We see that $x = -1$ and $x = 2$ are exact solutions of the equation.

EXERCISE 4-20

Solve each of the following two logarithmic and surd equations:

$$x^{3/2} \log(x) = x\log(x^{3/2}), \text{ sqrt[1-}x\text{]+sqrt[1+}x\text{]} = a.$$

```
>> maple('fsolve(x^(3/2)*log(x)=x*log(x)^(3/2))')
```

ans =

1.

Next we graph the function (see Figure 4-3) in order to find the intervals in which possible solutions may be found. This confirms that $x = 1$ is the only real solution.

```
>> fplot('[^(3/2) x * log(x), x * log(x) ^(3/2)]', [0.3, -1, 6])
```

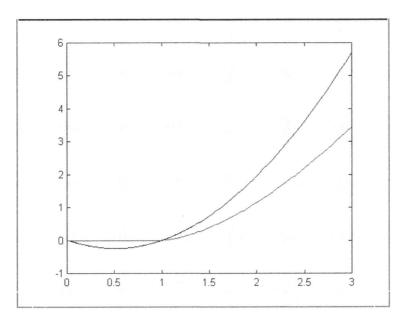

Figure 4-3.

Now, let's solve the surd equation:

```
>> pretty(sym(solve('sqrt(1-x)+sqrt(1+x)=a','x')))
```

$$\left[-\tfrac{1}{2}\, a\, (-a^2 + 4)^{1/2} \right]$$
$$\left[\tfrac{1}{2}\, a\, (-a^2 + 4)^{1/2} \right]$$

EXERCISE 4-21

Solve the following two equations:

$$x^5 + 16x^4 + 7x^3 + 17x^2 + 11x + 5 = 0 \text{ and } x^4 - 1 = 0.$$

In addition, solve the first equation modulo 19 and the second modulo 5.

```
>> s1=solve('x^5 +16*x^4+7*x^3+17*x^2+11*x+5=0')
```

```
[                        -15.61870451719182]
[-.3867059805744952-.3977796861292117*i]
[-.3867059805744952+.3977796861292117*i]
[ .1960582391704047-1.000858165543796*i]
[ .1960582391704047+1.000858165543796*i]
```

```
>> s2=solve('x^4-1=0')
```

s2 =

```
[1]
[-1]
[i]
[-i]
```

Now we find the modulo 19 solutions of the first equation:

```
>> maple('msolve(x^5 +16*x^4+7*x^3+17*x^2+11*x+5=0,19)')
```

ans =

{x = 1}, {x = 18}, {x = 3,} {x = 7}, {x = 12}

We calculate the modulo 5 solution of the second equation:

```
>> maple('msolve(x^4-1=0,5)')
```

ans =

{x = 1}, {x = 2}, {x = 3,} {x = 4}

Since the two equations are polynomial equations, we also have the option to solve them with the command *roots*. We have:

```
>> roots([5,11,17,7,16,5])
```

ans =

```
-1.2183 + 1.3164i
-1.2183 - 1.3164i
 0.2827 + 0.9302i
 0.2827 - 0.9302i
-0.3289
```

```
>> roots([-1,0,0,0,1])
```

ans =

```
-1.0000
 0.0000 + 1.0000i
 0.0000 - 1.0000i
 1.0000
```

EXERCISE 4-22

Solve the following system of two equations:

$$\cos(x/12)/\exp(x^2/16) = y$$

$$-5/4 + y = \sin(x^{3/2})$$

```
>> [x, y] = solve('cos(x/12) /exp(x^2/16) = y ',' - 5/4 + y = sin(x ^(3/2))')
```

x =

2.412335896593778

y =

.6810946557469383

EXERCISE 4-23

Find the intersection of the hyperbolas with equations $x^2 - y^2 = r^2$ and $a^2x^2 - b^2y^2 = a^2b^2$ with the parabola $z^2 = 2px$.

```
>> [x, y, z] = solve('a^2*x^2-b^2*y^2=a^2*b^2','x^2-y^2=r^2','z^2=2*p*x',  'x,y,z')
```

x =

*[1/2*RootOf((a^2-b^2)*_Z^4+4*b^2*r^2*p^2-4*a^2*b^2*p^2)^2/p]*
*[1/2*RootOf((a^2-b^2)*_Z^4+4*b^2*r^2*p^2-4*a^2*b^2*p^2)^2/p]*

y =

[1/2(RootOf((a^2-b^2)*_Z^4+4*b^2*r^2*p^2-4*a^2*b^2*p^2)^4-4*r^2*p^2)^(1/2)/p]*
[-1/2(RootOf((a^2-b^2)*_Z^4+4*b^2*r^2*p^2-4*a^2*b^2*p^2)^4-4*r^2*p^2)^(1/2)/p]*

z =

*[RootOf((a^2-b^2)*_Z^4+4*b^2*r^2*p^2-4*a^2*b^2*p^2)]*
*[RootOf((a^2-b^2)*_Z^4+4*b^2*r^2*p^2-4*a^2*b^2*p^2)]*

Now, we simplify the *RootOf* expression:

```
>> [simple(allvalues (x)), simple(allvalues (y)), simple(allvalues (z))]
```

ans =

```
[b*(-r^2+a^2) ^(1/2) /(a^2-b^2) ^(1/2) b]  [a *(b^2-r^2) ^(1/2) /(a^2-b^2) ^(1/2)]
[2 ^(1/2) * b ^(1/2) * p ^(1/2) *(-r^2+a^2) ^(1/4) /(a^2-b^2) ^(1/4)]
[b*(-r^2+a^2) ^(1/2) /(a^2-b^2) ^(1/2) b]  [a *(b^2-r^2) ^(1/2) /(a^2-b^2) ^(1/2)]
[- 2 ^(1/2) * b ^(1/2) * p ^(1/2) *(-r^2+a^2) ^(1/4) /(a^2-b^2) ^(1/4)]
[-b *(-r^2+a^2) ^(1/2) /(a^2-b^2) ^(1/2)]  [a *(b^2-r^2) ^(1/2) /(a^2-b^2) ^(1/2)]
[i * 2 ^(1/2) * b ^(1/2) * p ^(1/2) *(-r^2+a^2) ^(1/4) /(a^2-b^2) ^(1/4)]
[-b*(-r^2+a^2)^(1/2)/(a^2-b^2)^(1/2)]  [ a*(b^2-r^2)^(1/2)/(a^2-b^2)^(1/2)]
[-i*2^(1/2)*b^(1/2)*p^(1/2)*(-r^2+a^2)^(1/4)/(a^2-b^2)^(1/4)]
[ b*(-r^2+a^2)^(1/2)/(a^2-b^2)^(1/2)]  [-a*(b^2-r^2)^(1/2)/(a^2-b^2)^(1/2)]
[    2^(1/2)*b^(1/2)*p^(1/2)*(-r^2+a^2)^(1/4)/(a^2-b^2)^(1/4)]
[ b*(-r^2+a^2)^(1/2)/(a^2-b^2)^(1/2)]  [-a*(b^2-r^2)^(1/2)/(a^2-b^2)^(1/2)]
[   -2^(1/2)*b^(1/2)*p^(1/2)*(-r^2+a^2)^(1/4)/(a^2-b^2)^(1/4)]
[-b*(-r^2+a^2)^(1/2)/(a^2-b^2)^(1/2)]  [-a*(b^2-r^2)^(1/2)/(a^2-b^2)^(1/2)]
[ i*2^(1/2)*b^(1/2)*p^(1/2)*(-r^2+a^2)^(1/4)/(a^2-b^2)^(1/4)]
[-b*(-r^2+a^2)^(1/2)/(a^2-b^2)^(1/2)]  [-a*(b^2-r^2)^(1/2)/(a^2-b^2)^(1/2)]
[-i*2^(1/2)*b^(1/2)*p^(1/2)*(-r^2+a^2)^(1/4)/(a^2-b^2)^(1/4)]
```

Each line of this output (triple of values) is a solution of the system, i.e., a point of intersection of the three curves.

EXERCISE 4-24

Solve the inequality $x^2 + x > 5$.

```
>> maple('solve(x^2+x>5,x)')
```

ans =

```
RealRange(-inf,Open(-1/2-1/2*21^(1/2))),RealRange(Open(-1/2+1/2*21^(1/2)),inf)
```

4.7 Systems of Linear Equations

In the previous sections we have studied equations and systems in general. We will now focus on linear systems of equations. To solve such systems we could simply use the commands we have seen so far, however MATLAB has a selection of special commands designed especially for linear systems. We summarize these commands below.

> **linsolve(M,V)** solves the system **M&*x=V, where M is the matrix of the system and V is the vector of independent terms (number of elements of *V* = number of rows in *M*).**

> **linsolve (M1, M2) finds the matrix X such that M1&*X=M2. The dimensions of *M1, M2* and *X* must be compatible.**

> **linsolve(M,V,name,variable) solves the system *M&*x* = *V* and assigns the specified name to the rank of *M*. If Maple needs to name variables for solutions it will use the names *variable[1], variable[2],* etc. If the variable argument is not specified, Maple will use values _t[1], _t[2], etc. as variable names, if necessary.**

leastsqrs(M,V) finds the vector x satisfying the equation M&*x=V in the sense of least squares (x minimizes the *2-norm of M &*x--V*).

leastsqrs({equ1,...,equm},{var1,...,varn}) gives *var1,..., varn* that satisfies the given system of equations *equ1,..., equm* in the least squares sense.

Systems of linear equations can be converted to array form and solved using calculations with matrices. A system can be written in the form $M.X = B$, where X is the vector of variables, B the vector of independent terms and M the matrix of coefficients of the system. If M is a square matrix and the determinant of the matrix M is non-null, M is invertible, and the unique solution of the system can be written in the form: $X = M^{-1}B$. In this case, the commands *solve, linsolve, lscov, bicg, pcg, lsqr, gmr, gmres, minres, symmlq* or $M\backslash B$, already described above, offer the solution.

If the determinant of M is zero, the system has infinitely many solutions, since there are rows or columns in M that are linearly dependent. In this case, the number of redundant equations can be calculated to find out how many variables are needed to describe the solutions. If the matrix M is rectangular (not square), the system may be undetermined (the number of equations is less than the number of variables), overdetermined (the number of equations is greater than the number of variables) or non-singular (the number of equations is equal to number of variables and M has non-zero determinant). An indeterminate system can have infinitely many solutions, or none, and likewise for an overdetermined system. If a system has no solution, it is called inconsistent (incompatible), and if there is at least one solution, it is called consistent (compatible). The system $M . X = B$ is called *homogeneous* when the vector B is the null vector, i.e. the system is of the form $M . X = 0$. If the determinant of M is non-null, the unique solution of the system is the null vector (obtained with the command *linsolve*). If the determinant of M is zero, the system has infinitely many solutions. The solutions can be found using the commands *solve, linsolve, lsqr* or other commands described above for general linear systems.

Below is an example of a system with infinitely many solutions: $(x + 3y + 4z = 1, 2x + 3y + 3z = 1)$. In this case, MATLAB describes a parameterization of these solutions:

```
>> maple('solve({x+3*y+4*z=1, 2*x+3*y+3*z=1},{x,y,z})')
```

ans =

y = - 5/3 * z + 1/3, x = z, z = z

Any value of z will yield a solution of the system.

4.8 The Rouche-Frobenius Theorem

A fundamental tool in the analysis and solution of systems of equations is the *Rouche-Frobenius theorem*. This theorem says that a system of m equations with n unknowns has a solution if, and only if, the rank of the matrix of coefficients coincides with the rank of the array extended with the vector column of the system-independent terms. If the two ranks are equal, and equal to the number of unknowns, the system has a unique solution. If the two ranks are the same, but less than the number of unknowns, the system has infinitely many solutions. If they are different, the system has no solution.

In summary: Let A be the matrix of coefficients of the system and B the matrix A augmented by the column vector of independent terms.

If $rank(A)^1 rank(B)$, the system is incompatible (without solution).

If $rank (A) = rank(B) < n$, the system is indefinite (has infinitely many solutions).

If $= rank(A) = rank(B) = n$, the system has a unique solution.

This theorem allows us to analyze the solutions of a system of equations before solving it.

EXERCISE 4-25

Study and solve the system:

$$2x1 + x2 + x3 + x4 = 1$$

$$x1 + 2x2 + x3 + x4 = 1$$

$$x1 + x2 + 2 x3 + x4 = 1$$

$$x1 + x2 + x3 + 2x4 = 1$$

>> A = [2,1,1,1;1,2,1,1;1,1,2,1;1,1,1,2]

A =

```
2    1    1    1
1    2    1    1
1    1    2    1
1    1    1    2
```

>> B = [2,1,1,1,1;1,2,1,1,1;1,1,2,1,1;1,1,1,2,1]

B =

```
2    1    1    1    1
1    2    1    1    1
1    1    2    1    1
1    1    1    2    1
```

>> [rank(A), rank(B)]

ans =

4 4

We see that the matrix *A* and its augmented matrix *B* have rank 4, which, moreover, coincides with the number of unknowns. Therefore, the system has a unique solution. To calculate the solution, we use, for example, the command *linsolve*:

>> b = [1,1,1,1];

>> linsolve(A, b)

ans =

```
[1/5]
[1/5]
[1/5]
[1/5]
```

EXERCISE 4-26

Study and solve the system:

$$x1 - x2 + x3 = 1$$

$$4x1 + 5x2 - 5x3 = 4$$

$$2x1 + x2 - x3 = 2$$

$$x1 + 2x2 - 2x3 = 1$$

```
>> A = [1,-1,1;4,5,-5;2,1,-1;1,2,-2]
```

A =

```
1    -1     1
4     5    -5
2     1    -1
1     2    -2
```

```
>> B = [1,-1,1,1;4,5,-5,4;2,1,-1,2;1,2,-2,1]
```

B =

```
1    -1     1     1
4     5    -5     4
2     1    -1     2
1     2    -2     1
```

```
>> [rank(A), rank(B)]
```

ans =

2 2

We see that the rank of A and B coincide and its value is 2, which is less than the number of unknowns in the system (3). Therefore, the system will have infinitely many solutions. We try to solve it with the command *solve*:

```
>> maple('solve({x1-x2+x3=1,4*x1+5*x2-5*x3=4,2*x1+x2-x3=2,))
   x1+2*x2-2*x3=1}, {x1,x2,x3})')
```

ans =

{x 2 = x 3, x 1 = 1, x 3 = x 3}

Infinitely many solutions are obtained using the parameter $x3$, so that the set of solutions is given by $\{(1, x3, x3): x3 \in R\}$. Note that the trivial solution (1,0,0) is obtained by setting the parameter equal to zero.

The solution can also be found with the command *leastsqrs* as follows:

```
>> pretty(sym(maple('leastsqrs(array([[1,-1,1],[4,5,-5],[2,1,-1],[1,2,-2]]),
vector([1,4,2,1]))')))
```

$$1, \_t [1], \_t [1]$$

EXERCISE 4-27

Study and solve the system:

$$x + 2y + 3z = 6$$

$$x + 3y + 8z = 19$$

$$2x + 3y + z = -1$$

$$5x + 6y + 4z = 5$$

>> A = [1,2,3;1,3,8;2,3,1;5,6,4]

A =

```
1    2    3
1    3    8
2    3    1
5    6    4
```

>> B = [1,2,3,6;1,3,8,19;2,3,1,-1;5,6,4,5]

B =

```
1    2    3    6
1    3    8    19
2    3    1    -1
5    6    4    5
```

>> [rank(A), rank(B)]

ans =

3 3

We see that the ranks of *A* and *B* coincide and its value is 3, which is equal to the number of unknowns in the system. Therefore the system will have a unique solution. The only solution is obtained with the command *linsolve*:

>> maple('solve({x+2*y+3*z=6,x+3*y+8*z=19,2*x+3*y+z=-1, 5*x+6*y+4*z=5}, {x,y,z})')

ans =

x = 1, y = - 2,   z = 3

The solution also can be found with the command *linsolve* as follows:

>> pretty(sym(maple('linsolve(array([[1,2,3],[1,3,8],[2,3,1],[5,6,4]]), (((vector([6,19,-1,5]))')))

$$[1 \ -2 \ -3]$$

EXERCISE 4-28

Study and solve the system:

$$x + 2y + 3z + t = 6$$
$$x + 3y + 8z + t = 19$$

```
>> A = [1,2,3,1;1,3,8,1]
```

A =

```
1    2    3    1
1    3    8    1
```

```
>> B = [1,2,3,1,6;1,3,8,1,19]
```

B =

```
1    2    3    1    6
1    3    8    1    19
```

```
>> [rank(A), rank(B)]
```

ans =

2 2

We see that the rank of *A* and *B* coincide and its value is 2, which is less than the number of unknowns in the system (4). Therefore, the system has infinitely many solutions. We try to solve it:

```
>> maple('solve({x+2*y+3*z+t=6,x+3*y+8*z+t=19},{x,y,z,t})')
```

ans =

*{y = - 5 * z + 13, t = - x+7 * z-20, x = x, z = z}*

This time the solution depends on two parameters. As *z* and *t* vary over the real numbers, all the solutions of the system are obtained. These solutions form a two-dimensional subspace of four-dimensional real space.

The solution can also be found with the commands *leastsqrs* and *linsolve* as follows:

```
>> pretty(sym(maple('linsolve(array([[1,2,3,1],[1,3,8,1]]),vector([6,19]))')))
```

[_t[2], 13 - 5 _t[1], _t[1], -_t[2] - 20 + 7 _t[1]]

```
>> pretty(sym(maple('leastsqrs(array([[1,2,3,1],[1,3,8,1]]),vector([6,19]))')))
```

[_t [2],   13 - 5 _t [1],   _t [1], - _t [2] - 20 + 7 _t [1]]

EXERCISE 4-29

Study and solve the system:

$$x1 + 2x2 - x3 = 10$$
$$2x1 + 4x2 - 2x3 = 5$$
$$x1 + x2 + x3 = 6$$

```
>> A = [1,2,-1;2,4,-2;1,1,1]

A =

1    2    -1
2    4    -2
1    1     1

>> B = [1,2,-1,10;2,4,-2,5;1,1,1,6]

B =

1    2    -1    10
2    4    -2     5
1    1     1     6

>> [rank(A), rank(B)]

ans =

2 3
```

The rank of *A* is 2 and the rank of *B* is 3, therefore the system has no solution.

4.9 Homogeneous Systems

A system $A \cdot X = B$ is said to be homogeneous if the vector of independent terms B is null, so every homogeneous system will be of the form $A X = 0$.

In a homogeneous system, the rank of the matrix of coefficients and the rank of the matrix extended to include the independent terms in its final column always coincide. If we apply the Rouche-Frobenius theorem, a homogeneous system will have a unique solution when the determinant of the matrix A is non-zero. This unique solution is the null vector. A homogeneous system will have infinitely many solutions when the determinant of the matrix A is zero. In this case, the infinitely many solutions can be calculated as in general systems (using the command *solve*), or by using the function *nullspace(A)*.

EXERCISE 4-30

Study and solve the system:

$$x1 + 2x2 - x3 = 0$$

$$2x1 - x2 + x3 = 0$$

$$3x1 + x2 = 0$$

```
>> A = [1,2, - 1; 2, - 1, 1; 3,1,0]
```

A =

```
1   2 -1
2  -1 -1
3   1  0
```

```
>> det(A)
```

ans =

0

The system is homogeneous and the determinant of the matrix of coefficients is zero, so there are infinitely many solutions:

```
>> maple('solve({x1+2*x2-x3=0,2*x1-x2+x3=0,3*x1+x2=0},{x1,x2,x3})')
```

ans =

x2 = - 3 * x1, x3 = - 5 * x1, x1 = x1

The set of all solutions is obtained by varying the parameter *x1* over all real numbers.

If we apply the command *nullspace*, we obtain a basis of the kernel of the matrix of the system, i.e., a basis for the set of solutions of the system *a. X = 0*, which is precisely the homogeneous system that we want to solve. Therefore, the function *nullspace* gives a non-trivial solution of the homogeneous system.

```
>> nullspace(A)
```

ans =

```
[1]
[-3]
[-5]
```

This is the solution that corresponds to the value of the parameter *x1 = 1*.

The set of solutions is the set of linear combinations of the basis elements. In this case the basis is formed by a single vector, so the general solution is just a constant multiple of this vector, so the result matches that found by the general method.

EXERCISE 4-31

Study and solve the system:

$$3x1 + x2 + x3 - x4 = 0$$
$$2x1 + x2 - 3x + 4 = 0x$$
$$x1 + 2x2 + 4x3 + 2x4 = 0$$
$$2x1 + x2 - 2x3 - x4 = 0$$

```
>> det([3,1,1,-1;2,1,-1,1;1,2,4,2;2,1,-2,-1])
```

ans =

-30

As the determinant of the matrix of coefficients is non-zero, the system has only the trivial solution:

```
>> maple('solve({3*x1+x2+x3-x4=0,2*x1+x2-x3+x4=0,x1+2*x2-4*x3-2*x4=0,
x1-x2-3*x3-5*x4=0},{x1,x2,x3,x4})')
```

ans =

x4 = 0, x2 = 0, x3 = 0, x1 = 0

EXERCISE 4-32

Study and solve the following system of equations, according to the values of m:

$$mx + y + z = 1$$
$$x + my + z = m$$
$$x + y + mz = m \wedge 2$$

```
>> maple('A: = m - > array([[m,1,1],[1,m,1],[1,1,m]])');
```

We consider the matrix of coefficients of the system as a function of m and study its rank according to the values of m:

```
>> maple('solve (det (A (m)) = 0, m)')
```

ans =

-2, 1, 1

The values of m which determine the rank of the matrix are −2 and 1.

We now consider the augmented matrix as a function of m:

```
>> maple('B:=m->array([[m,1,1,1],[1,m,1,m],[1,1,m,m^2]])');
```

We will study the case $m = -2$:

```
>> maple('rank(A(-2))')
```

ans =

2

```
>> maple('rank(B(-2))')
```

ans =

3

We see that the ranks of the two matrices are different, hence the system has no solution for $m = -2$.

Now we study the case $m = 1$:

```
>> maple('rank(A(1))')
```

ans =

1

```
>> maple('rank(B(1))')
```

ans =

1

Now the rank of the two matrices is 1, which is less than the number of unknowns. Thus, the system has infinitely many solutions. We find them by substituting $m = 1$ into the initial system:

```
>> maple('solve(x+y+z=1,{x,y,z})')
```

x = -y-z + 1, y = y,   z = z

The infinite set of solutions is obtained by varying the parameters y and z over the real numbers.

In the case where m is different from -2 and -1, the system has a unique solution, which we find using the command *solve*:

```
>> pretty(sym(maple('solve({m*x+y+z=1,x+m*y+z=m,x+y+m*z=m^2}, {x,y,z})')))
```

$$\left\{ y = \frac{1}{m+2}, \; x = -\frac{m+1}{m+2}, \; z = \frac{m^2 + 2m + 1}{m+2} \right\}$$

EXERCISE 4-33

Study and solve the following system according to the values of *m*:

$$my = m$$

$$(1 + m)x - z = m$$

$$y + z = m$$

```
>> maple('A: = m - > array([[0,m,0],[m+1,0,-1],[0,1,1]])');
```

```
>> maple('solve(det(A (m)) = 0, m)')
```

ans =

-1, 0

We see that the values of *m* which determine the rank of the matrix of coefficients of the system are *m = 1* and *m = 0*.

We now consider the augmented matrix:

```
>> maple('B:=m->array([[0,m,0,m],[m+1,0,-1,m],[0,1,1,m]])');
```

```
>> maple('rank(A(-1))')
```

ans =

2

```
>> maple('rank(B(-1))')
```

ans =

3

If *m* = −1, we see that the system has no solution because the rank of the matrix of coefficients of the system is 2 and the rank of the augmented matrix is 3.

Now, we analyze the case *m* = 0:

When *m* is zero the system is homogeneous, since all the independent terms are all zero. We analyze the determinant of the matrix of coefficients of the system.

```
>> maple(det (A (0)))
```

ans =

0

Since the determinant is zero, the system has infinitely many solutions:

```
>> maple('solve({x-z=0,y+z=0},{x,y,z})')
```

ans =

```
z = z, y = - z, x = z
```

The infinite set of solutions is obtained by varying the parameter *z* over the real numbers.

If *m* is neither 0 nor –1, the system has a unique solution since the ranks of the matrix of the system and of the augmented matrix coincide. The solution can be found using the command *linsolve*.

```
>> pretty(sym(maple('solve({m * y= m,(1+m) * x-z = m, y + z = m}, {x, y, z})')))
```

$$\{y = 1, \ z = m - 1, \ x = \frac{2 \ m - 1}{m + 1}\}$$

EXERCISE 4-34

Study and solve the following system according to the values of *m*:

$$3x + 3y - z = 0$$
$$-4x - 2y + mz = 0$$
$$3x + 4y + 6z = 0$$

It is a homogeneous system, so we analyze the determinant of the matrix of coefficients:

```
>> maple('A: = m - > array([[3,3,-1],[-4,-2,m],[3,4,6]])');
```

```
>> maple('solve(det(A (m)) = 0, m)')
```

ans =

46/3

If *m* is different from 46/3, the system has only the trivial solution.

If *m* = *46/3*, the system has infinitely many solutions:

```
>> maple('solve({3*x+3*y-z=0,-4*x-2*y+46/3*z=0,3*x+4*y+6*z=0},{x,y,z})')
```

ans =

```
{z = - 1/7 * y, x = - 22/21 * y, y = y}
```

The infinite set of solutions is obtained by varying the parameter *y* over the real numbers.

CHAPTER 5

■ ■ ■

Vector and Matrix Functions of Complex Variables

5.1 Complex Numbers

MATLAB implements a simple way to work with complex numbers in binary form $a+bi$ or $a+bj$, representing the imaginary unit by means of the symbol i or j. Note that it is not necessary to include the product symbol (asterisk) before the imaginary unit, but if it is included, everything still works correctly. It is important, however, that spaces are not introduced between the imaginary unit i and its coefficient.

Complex numbers can have symbolic or numeric real or imaginary parts. Operations are carried out with a precision that is set by the command *format*. Thus, it is possible to work with complex numbers in exact rational format via the command *format rat*.

The common arithmetical operations with complex numbers (sum, difference, product, division and exponentiation) are carried out in the usual way. Examples are shown in Figure 5-1.

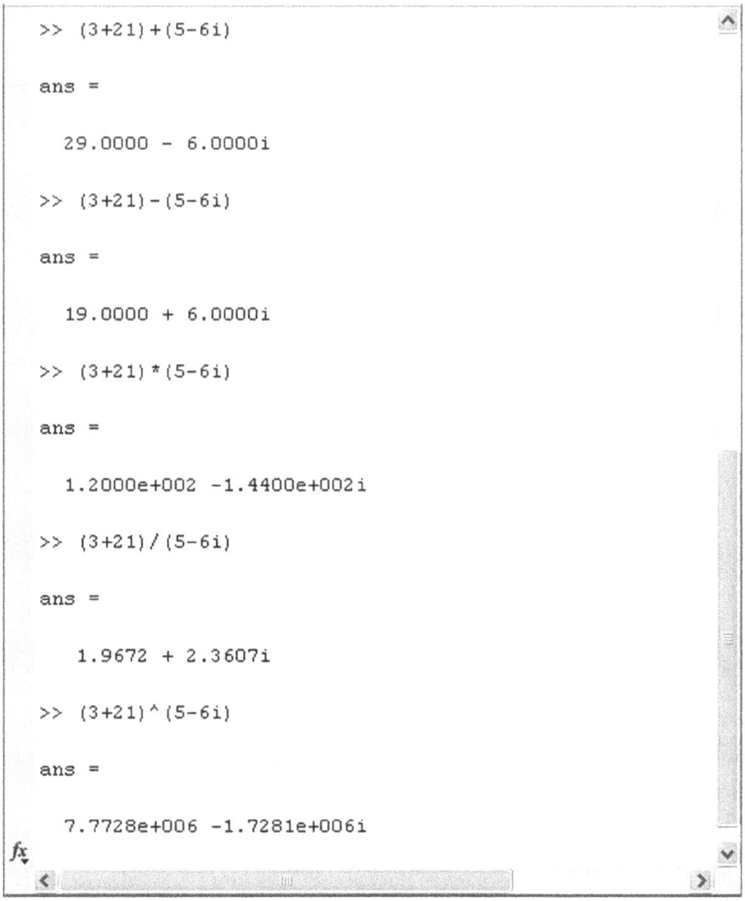

```
>> (3+21)+(5-6i)

ans =

   29.0000 - 6.0000i

>> (3+21)-(5-6i)

ans =

   19.0000 + 6.0000i

>> (3+21)*(5-6i)

ans =

   1.2000e+002 -1.4400e+002i

>> (3+21)/(5-6i)

ans =

    1.9672 + 2.3607i

>> (3+21)^(5-6i)

ans =

   7.7728e+006 -1.7281e+006i
```

Figure 5-1.

Obviously, as the real numbers are a subset of the complex numbers, any function of complex variables will also be valid for real variables.

5.2 General Functions of a Complex Variable

MATLAB has a range of preset general functions of a complex variable, which of course will also be valid for real, rational and integer variables. The following sections present the most important examples.

5.2.1 Trigonometric Functions of a Complex Variable

Below is a table summarizing the trigonometric functions of a complex variable and their inverses that are incorporated in MATLAB, illustrated with examples.

Function	Inverse
sin (z) *sine*	**asin (z)** *arc sine*
>> sin(5-6i)	>> asin(1-i)
ans =	ans =
-1 9343e + 002-5 7218e + 001i	0.6662 - 1.0613i
cos (z) *cosine*	**acos (z)** *arc cosine*
>> cos (3 + 4i)	>> acos (-i)
ans =	ans =
-27.0349 - 3.8512i	1.5708 + 0.8814i
tan (z) *tangent*	**atan(z) and atan2(imag(z),real(z))** *arc tangent*
>> tan(pi/4i)	>> atan(-pi*i)
ans =	ans =
0 - 0.6558i	1.5708 - 0.3298i
csc (z) *cosecant*	**acsc (z)** *arc cosecant*
>> csc(1-i)	>> acsc(2i)
ans =	ans =
0.6215 + 0.3039i	0 - 0.4812i

(continued)

Function	Inverse
sec (z) *secant*	**asec (z)** *arc secant*
>> sec(-i)	>> asec(0.6481+0i)
ans =	ans =
0.6481	0 + 0.9999i
cot (z) *cotangent*	**acot (z)** *arc cotangent*
>> cot(-j)	>> acot(1-6j)
ans =	ans =
0 + 1.3130i	0.0277 + 0.1635i

5.2.2 Hyperbolic Functions of a Complex Variable

Below is a table of hyperbolic functions of a complex variable and their inverses that are incorporated in MATLAB, illustrated with examples.

Function	Inverse
sinh(z) *hyperbolic sine*	**asinh(z)** *arc hyperbolic sine*
>> sinh(1+i)	>> asinh(0.6350 + 1.2985i)
ans =	ans =
0.6350 + 1.2985i	1.0000 + 1.0000i
cosh(z) *hyperbolic cosine*	**acosh(z)** *arc hyperbolic cosine*
>> cosh(1-i)	>> acosh(0.8337 - 0.9889i)
ans =	ans =
0.8337 - 0.9889i	1.0000 - 1.0000i

(continued)

Function	Inverse
tanh(z) *hyperbolic tangent*	**atanh(z)** *arc hyperbolic tangent*
>> tanh(3-5i)	>> atanh(3-41)
ans =	ans =
1.0042 + 0.0027i	-0.0263 - 1.5708i
csch(z) *hyperbolic cosecant*	**acsch(z)** *arc hyperbolic cosecant*
>> csch(i)	>> acsch(-1.1884i)
ans =	ans =
0 - 1.1884i	0 + 1.0000i
sech(z) *hyperbolic secant*	**asech(z)** *arc hyperbolic secant*
>> sech(i^i)	>> asech(5-0i)
ans =	ans =
0.9788	0 + 1.3694i
coth(z) *hyperbolic cotangent*	**acoth(z)** *arc hyperbolic cotangent*
>> coth(9+i)	>> acoth(1-i)
ans =	ans =
1.0000 - 0.0000i	0.4024 + 0.5536i

(*continued*)

5.2.3 Exponential and Logarithmic Functions of a Complex Variable

Below is a table summarizing the exponential and logarithmic functions that are incorporated in MATLAB, illustrated with examples.

Function	Meaning
exp (z)	*Exponential function to base e (e ^ x)*
	`>> exp(1-i)`
	`ans =`
	`1.4687 - 2.2874i`
log (x)	*Base e logarithm of x*
	`>> log(1.4687-2.2874i)`
	`ans =`
	`1.0000 - 1.0000i`
log10 (x)	*Base 10 logarithm of x*
	`>> log10(100 + 100i)`
	`ans =`
	`2.1505 + 0.3411i`
log2 (x)	*Base 2 logarithm of x*
	`>> log2(4-6i)`
	`ans =`
	`2.8502 - 1.4179i`

(continued)

Function	Meaning
pow2 (x)	*Base 2 power function (2^x)*
	`>> pow2(2.8502-1.4179i)`
	`ans =`
	`3.9998. - 6.0000i`
sqrt (x)	*Square root of x*
	`>> sqrt(1+i)`
	`ans =`
	`1.0987 + 0.4551i`

5.2.4 Specific Functions of a Complex Variable

MATLAB incorporates a specific group of functions of a complex variable which allow you to work with moduli, arguments, and real and imaginary parts. Among these features are the following:

Function	Meaning
abs (z)	*The modulus (absolute value) of z*
	`>> abs(12.425-8.263i)`
	`ans =`
	`14.9217`
angle (z)	*The argument of z*
	`>> angle(12.425-8.263i)`
	`ans =`
	`-0.5869`

(continued)

Function	Meaning
conj (z)	*The complex conjugate of z*
	`>> conj(12.425-8.263i)`
	`ans =`
	`12.4250 + 8.2630i`
real (z)	*The real part of z*
	`>> real(12.425-8.263i)`
	`ans =`
	`12.4250`
imag (z)	*The imaginary part of z*
	`>> imag(12.425-8.263i)`
	`ans =`
	`-8.2630`
floor (z)	*Applies the floor function to real(z) and imag(z)*
	`>> floor(12.425-8.263i)`
	`ans =`
	`12.0000 - 9.0000i`
ceil (z)	*Applies the ceiling function to real(z) and imag(z)*
	`>> ceil(12.425-8.263i)`
	`ans =`
	`13.0000 - 8.0000i`

(*continued*)

Function	Meaning
round (z)	*Applies the round function to real(z) and imag(z)*
	`>> round(12.425-8.263i)`
	`ans =`
	`12.0000 - 8.0000i`
fix (z)	*Applies the fix function to real(z) and imag(z)*
	`>> fix(12.425-8.263i)`
	`ans =`
	`12.0000 - 8.0000i`

5.3 Basic Functions with Complex Vector Arguments

MATLAB enables you to work with functions of a complex matrix or vector. Of course, these functions are also valid for real variables since the real numbers are included in the complex numbers. Below is a table summarizing the functions of complex vector variables that are incorporated in MATLAB. Later, when the functions of complex matrix variables are tabulated, we will observe that all of them are also valid for vector variables, a vector being a particular case of a matrix.

max (V)	*The maximum component of V. (max is calculated for complex vectors as the complex number with the largest complex modulus (magnitude), computed with max(abs(V)). Then it computes the largest phase angle with max(angle(V)), if necessary.)*
	`>> max([1-i 1+i 3-5i 6i])`
	`ans =`
	`0 + 6.0000i`
	`>> max ([1, 0, -23, 12, 16])`
	`ans =`
	`16`

(continued)

min (V)	*The minimum component of V. (min is calculated for complex vectors as the complex number with the smallest complex modulus (magnitude), computed with min(abs(V)). Then it computes the smallest phase angle with min(angle(V)), if necessary.)*

```
>> min([1-i 1+i 3-5i 6i])

ans =

1.0    -1.0000i

>> min ([1, 0, -23, 12, 16])

ans =

-23
```

mean (V)	*Average of the components of V.*

```
>> mean([1-i 1+i 3-5i 6i])

ans =

1.2500 + 0.2500i

>> mean ([1, 0, -23, 12, 16])

ans =

1.2000
```

median (V)	*Median of the components of V.*

```
>> median([1-i 1+i 3-5i 6i])

ans =

2.0000 - 2.0000i

>> median ([1, 0, -23, 12, 16])

ans =

1
```

(*continued*)

std (V)   *Standard deviation of the components of V.*

>> std([1-i 1+i 3-5i 6i])

ans =

4.7434

>> std ([1, 0, -23, 12, 16])

ans =

15.1888

sort (V)   *Sorts the components of V in ascending order. For complex entries the order is by absolute value and argument.*

>> sort([1-i 1+i 3-5i 6i])

ans =

Columns 1 through 2

1.0000 - 1.0000i   1.0000 + 1.0000i

Columns 3 through 4

3.0000 - 5.0000i   0 + 6 0000i

>> sort ([1, 0, -23, 12, 16])

ans =

-23 0 1 12 16

(*continued*)

sum (V)	*Returns the sum of the components of V.*

```
>> sum([1-i 1+i 3-5i 6i])

ans =

5.0000 + 1.0000i

>> sum ([1, 0, -23, 12, 16])

ans =

6
```

prod (V)	*Returns the product of the components of V, so, for example, n! = prod(1:n).*

```
>> prod([1-i 1+i 3-5i 6i])

ans =

60.0000 + 36 0000i

>> prod ([1, 0, -23, 12, 16])

ans =

0
```

(*continued*)

cumsum (V)   *Gives the cumulative sums of the components of V.*

```
>> cumsum([1-i 1+i 3-5i 6i])

ans =

Columns 1 through 2

1.0000 - 1.0000i    2.0000

Columns 3 through 4

5.0000 - 5.0000i 5.0000 + 1.0000i

>> cumsum ([1, 0, -23, 12, 16])

ans =

1 1 -22 -10 -6
```

cumprod (V)   *Gives the cumulative products of the components of V.*

```
>> cumprod([1-i 1+i 3-5i 6i])

ans =

Columns 1 through 2

1.0000 - 1.0000i    2.0000

Columns 3 through 4

6.0000 - 10.0000i 60.0000 + 36 0000i

>> cumprod ([1, 0, -23, 12, 16])

ans =

1    0    0    0    0
```

(*continued*)

diff (V)	*Gives the vector of first differences of V (V_t - V_{t-1}).*

```
>> diff([1-i 1+i 3-5i 6i])

ans =

0 + 2.0000i   2.0000 - 6.0000i  -3.0000 + 11.0000i

>> diff([1, 0, -23, 12, 16])

ans =

-1-23 35 4
```

gradient (V)	*Gives the gradient of V.*

```
>> gradient([1-i 1+i 3-5i 6i])

ans =

Columns 1 through 3

0 + 2.0000i   1.0000 - 2.0000i  -0.5000 + 2.5000i

Column 4

-3,0000 + 11 0000i

>> gradient ([1, 0, -23, 12, 16])

ans =

-1.0000 - 12.0000 6.0000 19.5000 4.0000
```

(continued)

del2 (V)   *Gives the Laplacian of V (5-point discrete).*

```
>> del2([1-i 1+i 3-5i 6i])

ans =

Columns 1 through 3

2.2500 - 8.2500i    0.5000 - 2.0000i   -1.2500 + 4.2500i

Column 4

-3,0000 + 10 5000i

>> del2 ([1, 0, -23, 12, 16])

ans =

-25.5000 - 5.5000 14.5000 - 7.7500 - 30.0000
```

fft (V)   *Gives the discrete Fourier transform of V.*

```
>> fft([1-i 1+i 3-5i 6i])

ans =

Columns 1 through 3

5.0000 + 1.0000i  -7.0000 + 3.0000i    3.0000 - 13.0000i

Column 4

3.0000 + 5.0000i

>> fft([1, 0, -23, 12, 16])

ans =

Columns 1 through 3

6.0000              14.8435 +35.7894i -15.3435 -23.8824i

Columns 4 through 5

-15.3435 +23.8824i   14.8435 -35.7894i
```

(continued)

fft2 (V)   *Gives the two-dimensional discrete Fourier transform of V.*

```
>> fft2([1-i 1+i 3-5i 6i])

ans =

Columns 1 through 3

5.0000 + 1.0000i   -7.0000 + 3.0000i    3.0000 - 13.0000i

Column 4

3.0000 + 5.0000i

>> fft2([1, 0, -23, 12, 16])

ans =

Columns 1 through 3

6.0000             14.8435 +35.7894i -15.3435 -23.8824i

Columns 4 through 5

-15.3435 +23.8824i  14.8435 -35.7894i
```

(continued)

ifft (V)   *Gives the inverse discrete Fourier transform of V.*

```
>> ifft([1-i 1+i 3-5i 6i])

ans =

Columns 1 through 3

1.2500 + 0.2500i    0.7500 + 1.2500i    0.7500 - 3.2500i

Column 4

-1.7500 + 0.7500i

>> ifft([1, 0, -23, 12, 16])

ans =

Columns 1 through 3

1.2000 2.9687 - 7.1579i   -3.0687 + 4.7765i

Columns 4 through 5

-3.0687 - 4.7765i    2.9687 + 7.1579i
```

(continued)

ifft2 (V)   *Gives the inverse two-dimensional discrete Fourier transform of V.*

```
>> ifft2([1-i 1+i 3-5i 6i])

ans =

Columns 1 through 3

1.2500 + 0.2500i   0.7500 + 1.2500i   0.7500 - 3.2500i

Column 4

-1.7500 + 0.7500i

>> ifft2([1, 0, -23, 12, 16])

ans =

Columns 1 through 3

1.2000 2.9687 - 7.1579i  -3.0687 + 4.7765i

Columns 4 through 5

-3.0687 - 4.7765i   2.9687 + 7.1579i
```

5.4 Basic Functions with Complex Matrix Arguments

The functions given in the above table also support complex matrices as arguments, in which case the result is a row vector whose components are the results of applying the function to each column of the matrix. Let us not forget that these functions are also valid for real variables, since the set of real numbers is a subset of the set of complex numbers.

max (Z)   *Returns a row vector indicating the maximum component of each column of the matrix Z. (max is calculated for complex vectors V as the complex number with the largest complex modulus (magnitude), computed with max(abs(V)). Then it computes the largest phase angle with max(angle(V)), if necessary.)*

```
>> Z = [1-i 3i 5;-1+i 0 2i;6-5i 8i -7]

Z =

  1.0000 - 1.0000i        0 + 3.0000i   5.0000
 -1.0000 + 1.0000i        0             0 + 2.0000i
  6.0000 - 5.0000i        0 + 8.0000i  -7.0000

>> Z = [1-i 3i 5-12i;-1+i 0 2i;6-5i 8i -7+6i]

Z =

  1.0000 - 1.0000i        0 + 3.0000i   5.0000 - 12.0000i
 -1.0000 + 1.0000i        0                  0 +  2.0000i
  6.0000 - 5.0000i        0 + 8.0000i  -7.0000 +  6.0000i

>> max(Z)

ans =

  6.0000 - 5.0000i        0 + 8.0000i   5.0000 - 12.0000i

>> Z1 = [1 3 5;-1 0 2;6 8 -7]

Z1 =

   1    3    5
  -1    0    2
   6    8   -7

>> max(Z1)

ans =

   6    8    5
```

(*continued*)

min (Z)	*Returns a row vector indicating the minimum component of each column of the matrix Z. (min is calculated for complex vectors V as the complex number with the smallest complex modulus (magnitude), computed with min(abs(V)). Then it computes the smallest phase angle with min(angle(V)), if necessary.)*

```
>> min(Z)

ans =

1.0000 - 1.0000i        0                   0 + 2.0000i

>> min(Z1)

ans =

-1     0    -7
```

mean (Z)	*Returns a row vector indicating the mean of the components of each column of Z.*

```
>> mean(Z)

ans =

2.0000 - 1.6667i       0 + 3.6667i   -0.6667 - 1.3333i

>> mean(Z1)

ans =

2.0000    3.6667          0
```

(*continued*)

median (Z)   *Returns a row vector indicating the median of the components of each column of Z.*

```
>> median(Z)

ans =

-1.0000 + 1.0000i       0 + 3.0000i  -7.0000 + 6.0000i

>> median(Z1)

ans =

1    3    2
```

std (Z)   *Returns a row vector indicating the standard deviation of the components of each column of Z.*

```
>> std(Z)

ans =

4.7258    4.0415    11.2101

>> std(Z1)

ans =

3.6056    4.0415    6.2450
```

(*continued*)

sort (Z)   *Sorts the components of the columns of Z in ascending order. For complex entries the order is by absolute value and argument.*

```
>> sort(Z)

ans =

  1.0000 - 1.0000i       0                  0 +  2.0000i
 -1.0000 + 1.0000i       0 + 3.0000i   -7.0000 +  6.0000i
  6.0000 - 5.0000i       0 + 8.0000i    5.0000 - 12.0000i

>> sort(Z1)

ans =

  -1    0   -7
   1    3    2
   6    8    5
```

sum (Z)   *Returns a row vector indicating the sum of the components of each column of Z.*

```
>> sum(Z)

ans =

  6.0000 - 5.0000i       0 + 11.0000i   -2.0000 - 4.0000i

>> sum(Z1)

ans =

   6    11    0
```

(*continued*)

prod (Z)   *Returns a row vector indicating the product of the components of each column of Z.*

```
>> prod(Z)

ans =

1.0e+002 *

0.1000 + 0.1200i          0          -2.2800 + 0.7400i

>> prod(Z1)

ans =

-6     0    -70
```

cumsum (Z)   *Returns a matrix indicating the cumulative sums of the elements in the columns of Z.*

```
>> cumsum(Z)

ans =

1.0000 - 1.0000i      0 +  3.0000i   5.0000 - 12.0000i
0                     0 +  3.0000i   5.0000 - 10.0000i
6.0000 - 5.0000i      0 + 11.0000i  -2.0000 -  4.0000i

>> cumsum(Z1)

ans =

1     3     5
0     3     7
6    11     0
```

(*continued*)

cumprod(V)   *Returns a matrix indicating the cumulative products of the elements in the columns of Z.*

```
>> cumprod(Z)

ans =

1.0e+002 *

0.0100 - 0.0100i      0 + 0.0300i    0.0500 - 0.1200i
0        + 0.0200i      0              0.2400 + 0.1000i
0.1000 + 0.1200i      0             -2.2800 + 0.7400i

>> cumprod(Z1)

ans =

    1    3    5
   -1    0   10
   -6    0  -70
```

diff (Z)   *Returns the matrix of first differences of the components of the columns of Z.*

```
>> diff(Z)

ans =

-2.0000 + 2.0000i      0 - 3.0000i  -5.0000 + 14.0000i
 7.0000 - 6.0000i      0 + 8.0000i  -7.0000 +  4.0000i

>> diff(Z1)

ans =

   -2   -3   -3
    7    8   -9
```

(*continued*)

gradient (Z)   *Returns the matrix of gradients for the columns of Z.*

```
>> gradient(Z)

ans =

-1.0000 +  4.0000i   2.0000 - 5.5000i   5.0000 - 15.0000i
 1.0000 -  1.0000i   0.5000 + 0.5000i        0 +  2.0000i
-6.0000 + 13.0000i  -6.5000 + 5.5000i  -7.0000 -  2.0000i

>> gradient(Z1)

ans =

2.0000    2.0000    2.0000
1.0000    1.5000    2.0000
2.0000 -  6.5000 - 15.0000
```

del2 (Z)   *Returns the matrix indicating the Laplacian of the columns of Z (5-point discrete).*

```
>> del2(Z)

ans =

3.7500 - 6.7500i   1.5000 - 2.0000i   1.0000 - 7.2500i
2.0000 - 1.2500i  -0.2500 + 3.5000i  -0.7500 - 1.7500i
2.0000 - 5.7500i  -0.2500 - 1.0000i  -0.7500 - 6.2500i

>> del2(Z1)

ans =

 2.2500    2.7500   -1.5000
 2.5000    3.0000   -1.2500
-2.0000   -1.5000   -5.7500
```

(continued)

fft (Z)   *Returns the matrix with discrete Fourier transforms of the columns of Z.*

```
>> fft(Z)

ans =

  6.0000 - 5.0000i         0 + 11.0000i  -2.0000 -   4.0000i
  3.6962 + 7.0622i   -6.9282 -  1.0000i   5.0359 -  22.0622i
 -6.6962 - 5.0622i    6.9282 -  1.0000i  11.9641 -   9.9378i

>> fft(Z1)

ans =

  6.0000               11.0000                   0
 -1.5000 + 6.0622i    -1.0000 + 6.9282i   7.5000 -  7.7942i
 -1.5000 - 6.0622i    -1.0000 - 6.9282i   7.5000 +  7.7942i
```

fft2 (Z)   *Returns the matrix with the two-dimensional discrete Fourier transforms of the columns of the matrix Z.*

```
>> fft2(Z)

ans =

  4.0000 +  2.0000i  19.9904 - 10.2321i   -5.9904 - 6.7679i
  1.8038 - 16.0000i  22.8827 + 28.9545i  -13.5981 + 8.2321i
 12.1962 - 16.0000i  -8.4019 +  4.7679i  -23.8827 - 3.9545i

>> fft2(Z1)

ans =

 17.0000               0.5000 -  9.5263i   0.5000 +  9.5263i
  5.0000 + 5.1962i     8.0000 + 13.8564i -17.5000 -  0.8660i
  5.0000 - 5.1962i   -17.5000 +  0.8660i   8.0000 - 13.8564i
```

(continued)

ifft (Z)   *Returns the matrix with the inverse inverse discrete Fourier transform of the columns of the matrix Z.*

```
>> ifft(Z)

ans =

   2.0000 - 1.6667i        0 + 3.6667i  -0.6667 - 1.3333i
  -2.2321 - 1.6874i   2.3094 - 0.3333i   3.9880 - 3.3126i
   1.2321 + 2.3541i  -2.3094 - 0.3333i   1.6786 - 7.3541i

>> ifft(Z1)

ans =

   2.0000              3.6667                    0
  -0.5000 - 2.0207i  -0.3333 - 2.3094i   2.5000 + 2.5981i
  -0.5000 + 2.0207i  -0.3333 + 2.3094i   2.5000 - 2.5981i
```

ifft2 (Z)   *Returns the matrix with the inverse two-dimensional discrete Fourier transform of the columns of Z.*

```
>> ifft2(Z)

ans =

  0.4444 + 0.2222i  -0.6656 - 0.7520i   2.2212 - 1.1369i
  1.3551 - 1.7778i  -2.6536 - 0.4394i  -0.9335 + 0.5298i
  0.2004 - 1.7778i  -1.5109 + 0.9147i   2.5425 + 3.2172i

>> ifft2(Z1)

ans =

  1.8889              0.0556 + 1.0585i   0.0556 - 1.0585i
  0.5556 - 0.5774i   0.8889 - 1.5396i  -1.9444 + 0.0962i
  0.5556 + 0.5774i  -1.9444 - 0.0962i   0.8889 + 1.5396i
```

5.5 General Functions with Complex Matrix Arguments

MATLAB incorporates a broad group of hyperbolic, trigonometric, exponential and logarithmic functions that support a complex matrix as an argument. Obviously, all these functions also accept a complex vector as the argument, since a vector is a particular case of matrix. All functions are applied elementwise in the matrix.

5.5.1 Trigonometric Functions of a Complex Matrix Variable

Below is a table summarizing the trigonometric functions of a complex variable and their inverses which are incorporated in MATLAB, illustrated with examples. All the examples use as arguments the matrices Z and Z1 introduced at the beginning of the table in the description of the sine function.

Direct Trigonometric Functions

---

sin(Z) *sine function*

```
>> Z = [1-i, 1+i, 2i;3-6i, 2+4i, -i;i,2i,3i]

Z =

1.0000 - 1.0000i    1.0000 + 1.0000i         0 + 2.0000i
3.0000 - 6.0000i    2.0000 + 4.0000i         0 - 1.0000i
        0 + 1.0000i          0 + 2.0000i      0 + 3.0000i

>> Z1 = [1,1,2;3,2,-1;1,2,3]

Z1 =

1     1     2
3     2    -1
1     2     3

>> sin(Z)

ans =

1.0e+002 *

0.0130 - 0.0063i    0.0130 + 0.0063i        0 + 0.0363i
0.2847 + 1.9969i    0.2483 - 0.1136i        0 - 0.0118i
        0 + 0.0118i         0 + 0.0363i     0 + 0.1002i

>> sin(Z1)

ans =

0.8415 0.8415    0.9093
0.1411 0.9093 -  0.8415
0.8415 0.9093    0.1411
```

(continued)

Direct Trigonometric Functions

cos (Z) *cosine function*

```
>> cos(Z)

ans =

1.0e+002 *

 0.0083 + 0.0099i   0.0083 - 0.0099i   0.0376
-1.9970 + 0.2847i  -0.1136 - 0.2481i   0.0154
 0.0154             0.0376             0.1007

>> cos(Z1)

ans =

 0.5403    0.5403 - 0.4161
-0.9900 - 0.4161    0.5403
 0.5403 - 0.4161 - 0.9900
```

tan (Z) *tangent function*

```
>> tan(Z)

ans =

 0.2718 - 1.0839i   0.2718 + 1.0839i       0 + 0.9640i
-0.0000 - 1.0000i  -0.0005 + 1.0004i       0 - 0.7616i
 0       + 0.7616i       0 + 0.9640i       0 + 0.9951i

>> tan(Z1)

ans =

 1.5574    1.5574 - 2.1850
-0.1425 - 2.1850 - 1.5574
 1.5574 - 2.1850 - 0.1425
```

(continued)

Direct Trigonometric Functions

csc (Z) *cosecant function*

```
>> csc(Z)

ans =

0.6215 + 0.3039i    0.6215 - 0.3039i       0 - 0.2757i
0.0007 - 0.0049i    0.0333 + 0.0152i       0 + 0.8509i
     0 - 0.8509i         0 - 0.2757i       0 - 0.0998i

>> csc(Z1)

ans =

1.1884    1.1884    1.0998
7.0862    1.0998   -1.1884
1.1884    1.0998    7.0862
```

sec (Z) *secant function*

```
>> sec(Z)

ans =

 0.4983 - 0.5911i    0.4983 + 0.5911i    0.2658
-0.0049 - 0.0007i   -0.0153 + 0.0333i    0.6481
 0.6481                  0.2658           0.0993

>> sec(Z1)

ans =

 1.8508    1.8508   -2.4030
-1.0101   -2.4030    1.8508
 1.8508   -2.4030   -1.0101
```

(continued)

184

Direct Trigonometric Functions

cot (Z) *cotangent function*

```
>> cot(Z)

ans =

 0.2176 + 0.8680i    0.2176 - 0.8680i        0 - 1.0373i
-0.0000 + 1.0000i   -0.0005 - 0.9996i        0 + 1.3130i
      0 - 1.3130i          0 - 1.0373i        0 - 1.0050i

>> cot(Z1)

ans =

 0.6421     0.6421    -0.4577
-7.0153    -0.4577    -0.6421
 0.6421    -0.4577    -7.0153
```

Inverse Trigonometric Functions

asin (Z) *arc sine function*

```
>> asin(Z)

ans =

0.6662 - 1.0613i    0.6662 + 1.0613i        0 + 1.4436i
0.4592 - 2.5998i    0.4539 + 2.1986i        0 - 0.8814i
      0 + 0.8814i          0 + 1.4436i        0 + 1.8184i

>> asin(Z1)

ans =

1.5708                1.5708              1.5708 - 1.3170i
1.5708 - 1.7627i    1.5708 - 1.3170i    -1.5708
1.5708                1.5708 - 1.3170i    1.5708 - 1.7627i
```

(continued)

185

Inverse Trigonometric Functions

acos (Z) *arc cosine function*

```
>> acos(Z)

ans =

0.9046 + 1.0613i   0.9046 - 1.0613i   1.5708 - 1.4436i
1.1115 + 2.5998i   1.1169 - 2.1986i   1.5708 + 0.8814i
1.5708 - 0.8814i   1.5708 - 1.4436i   1.5708 - 1.8184i

>> acos(Z1)

ans =

0                  0                  0 + 1.3170i
0 + 1.7627i    0 + 1.3170i    3.1416
0                  0 + 1. 3170i    0 + 1. 7627i
```

atan(Z) and **atan2 (real(Z),imag(Z))** *arc tangent function*

```
>> atan(Z)

ans =

1.0172 - 0.4024i   1.0172 + 0.4024i   -1.5708 + 0.5493i
1.5030 - 0.1335i   1.4670 + 0.2006i        0 -      Infi
0     +     Infi  -1.5708 + 0.5493i  -1.5708 + 0.3466i

>> atan(Z1)

ans =

0.7854    0.7854    1.1071
1.2490    1.1071   -0.7854
0.7854    1.1071    1.2490
```

(continued)

Inverse Trigonometric Functions

acsc (Z) *arc cosecant function*

```
>> acsc(Z)

ans =

0.4523 + 0.5306i   0.4523 - 0.5306i       0 - 0.4812i
0.0661 + 0.1332i   0.0982 - 0.1996i       0 + 0.8814i
     0 - 0.8814i        0 - 0.4812i       0 - 0.3275i

>> acsc(Z1)

ans =

1.5708     1.5708     0.5236
0.3398     0.5236    -1.5708
1.5708     0.5236     0.3398
```

asec (Z) *arc secant function*

```
>> asec(Z)

ans =

1.1185 - 0.5306i   1.1185 + 0.5306i   1.5708 + 0.4812i
1.5047 - 0.1332i   1.4726 + 0.1996i   1.5708 - 0.8814i
1.5708 + 0.8814i   1.5708 + 0.4812i   1.5708 + 0.3275i

>> asec(Z1)

ans =

     0          0     1.0472
1.2310     1.0472     3.1416
     0     1.0472     1.2310
```

(continued)

Inverse Trigonometric Functions

---

acot (Z) *arc cotangent function*

```
>> acot(Z)

ans =

0.5536 + 0.4024i    0.5536 - 0.4024i        0 - 0.5493i
0.0678 + 0.1335i    0.1037 - 0.2006i        0 +    Infi
     0 -    Infi         0 - 0.5493i        0 - 0.3466i

>> acot(Z1)

ans =

0.7854    0.7854    0.4636
0.3218    0.4636   -0.7854
0.7854    0.4636    0.3218
```

5.5.2 Hyperbolic Functions of a Complex Matrix Variable

Below is a table summarizing the hyperbolic functions of complex matrix variables and their inverses which are incorporated in MATLAB, illustrated with examples.

Direct Hyperbolic Functions

---

sinh (Z) *hyperbolic sine function*

```
>> sinh (Z)

ans =

0.6350 - 1.2985i    0.6350 + 1.2985i        0 + 0.9093i
9.6189 + 2.8131i   -2.3707 - 2.8472i        0 - 0.8415i
     0 + 0.8415i         0 + 0.9093i        0 + 0.1411i

>> sinh(Z1)

ans =

 1.1752    1.1752    3.6269
10.0179    3.6269   -1.1752
 1.1752    3.6269   10.0179
```

(continued)

Direct Hyperbolic Functions

cosh (Z) *hyperbolic cosine function*

```
>> cosh(Z)

ans =

0.8337 - 0.9889i   0.8337 + 0.9889i  -0.4161
9.6667 + 2.7991i  -2.4591 - 2.7448i   0.5403
0.5403                 -0.4161            -0.9900

>> cosh(Z1)

ans =

 1.5431    1.5431    3.7622
10.0677    3.7622    1.5431
 1.5431    3.7622   10.0677
```

tanh (Z) *hyperbolic tangent function*

```
>> tanh(Z)

ans =

1.0839 - 0.2718i   1.0839 + 0.2718i        0 - 2.1850i
0.9958 + 0.0026i   1.0047 + 0.0364i        0 - 1.5574i
0        + 1.5574i        0 - 2.1850i        0 - 0.1425i

>> tanh(Z1)

ans =

0.7616    0.7616    0.9640
0.9951    0.9640   -0.7616
0.7616    0.9640    0.9951
```

(*continued*)

Direct Hyperbolic Functions

csch (z) *hyperbolic cosecant function*

```
>> csch (Z)

ans =

0.3039 + 0.6215i    0.3039 - 0.6215i       0 - 1.0998i
0.0958 - 0.0280i   -0.1727 + 0.2074i       0 + 1.1884i
0       - 1.1884i        0 - 1.0998i       0 - 7.0862i

>> csch(Z1)

ans =

0.8509    0.8509    0.2757
0.0998    0.2757   -0.8509
0.8509    0.2757    0.0998
```

sech (Z) *hyperbolic secant function*

```
>> sech (Z)

ans =

0.4983 + 0.5911i    0.4983 - 0.5911i   -2.4030
0.0954 - 0.0276i   -0.1811 + 0.2021i    1.8508
1.8508              -2.4030             -1.0101

>> sech(Z1)

ans =

0.6481    0.6481    0.2658
0.0993    0.2658    0.6481
0.6481    0.2658    0.0993
```

(*continued*)

Direct Hyperbolic Functions

coth (Z) *hyperbolic cotangent function*

```
>> coth (Z)

ans =

0.8680 + 0.2176i   0.8680 - 0.2176i      0 + 0.4577i
1.0042 - 0.0027i   0.9940 - 0.0360i      0 + 0.6421i
0        - 0.6421i      0 + 0.4577i      0 + 7.0153i

>> coth(Z1)

ans =

1.3130    1.3130    1.0373
1.0050    1.0373   -1.3130
1.3130    1.0373    1.0050
```

Inverse Hyperbolic Functions

asinh (Z) *hyperbolic arc sine function*

```
>> asinh(Z)

ans =

1.0613 - 0.6662i   1.0613 + 0.6662i   1.3170 + 1.5708i
2.5932 - 1.1027i   2.1836 + 1.0969i        0 - 1.5708i
0      + 1.5708i   1.3170 + 1.5708i   1.7627 + 1.5708i

>> asinh(Z1)

ans =

0.8814    0.8814    1.4436
1.8184    1.4436   -0.8814
0.8814    1.4436    1.8184
```

(continued)

191

Inverse Hyperbolic Functions

acosh (Z) *hyperbolic arc cosine function*

```
>> acosh(Z)

ans =

1.0613 - 0.9046i   1.0613 + 0.9046i   1.4436 + 1.5708i
2.5998 - 1.1115i   2.1986 + 1.1169i   0.8814 - 1.5708i
0.8814 + 1.5708i   1.4436 + 1.5708i   1.8184 + 1.5708i

>> acosh(Z1)

ans =

     0                 0           1.3170
 1.7627             1.3170             0 + 3.1416i
     0             1.3170           1.7627
```

atanh (Z) *hyperbolic arc tangent function*

```
>> atanh(Z)

ans =

0.4024 - 1.0172i   0.4024 + 1.0172i        0 + 1.1071i
0.0656 - 1.4377i   0.0964 + 1.3715i        0 - 0.7854i
0      + 0.7854i        0 + 1.1071i        0 + 1.2490i

>> atanh(Z1)

ans =

   inf               inf         0.5493 + 1.5708i
0.3466 + 1.5708i   0.5493 + 1.5708i    -inf
   inf             0.5493 + 1.5708i   0.3466 + 1.5708i
```

(continued)

Inverse Hyperbolic Functions

acsch (Z) *hyperbolic arc cosecant function*

```
>> acsch(Z)

ans =

0.5306 + 0.4523i   0.5306 - 0.4523i        0 - 0.5236i
0.0672 + 0.1334i   0.1019 - 0.2003i        0 + 1.5708i
0      - 1.5708i        0 - 0.5236i        0 - 0.3398i

>> acsch(Z1)

ans =

0.8814    0.8814    0.4812
0.3275    0.4812   -0.8814
0.8814    0.4812    0.3275
```

asech (Z) *hyperbolic arc secant function*

```
>> asech(Z)

ans =

0.5306 + 1.1185i   0.5306 - 1.1185i   0.4812 - 1.5708i
0.1332 + 1.5047i   0.1996 - 1.4726i   0.8814 + 1.5708i
0.8814 - 1.5708i   0.4812 - 1.5708i   0.3275 - 1.5708i

>> asech(Z1)

ans =

0              0              0 + 1.0472i
0 + 1.2310i    0 + 1.0472i    0 + 3.1416i
0              0 + 1.0472i    0 + 1.2310i
```

(continued)

193

Inverse Hyperbolic Functions

acoth (Z) *hyperbolic arc cotangent function*

```
>> acoth(Z)

ans =

0.4024 + 0.5536i    0.4024 - 0.5536i        0 - 0.4636i
0.0656 + 0.1331i    0.0964 - 0.1993i        0 + 0.7854i
0        - 0.7854i          0 - 0.4636i     0 - 0.3218i

>> acoth(Z1)

ans =

   Inf      Inf     0.5493
0.3466    0.5493     -Inf
   Inf    0.5493    0.3466
```

5.5.3 Exponential and Logarithmic Functions of Complex Matrix Variables

Below is a table summarizing the exponential and logarithmic functions which are incorporated in MATLAB, illustrated with examples. The matrices Z1 and Z are the same as those in the previous examples.

Function	Meaning
exp (Z)	*Base e exponential function (e ^ x)*

```
>> exp(Z)

ans =

  1.4687 - 2.2874i    1.4687 + 2.2874i   -0.4161 + 0.9093i
 19.2855 + 5.6122i   -4.8298 - 5.5921i    0.5403 - 0.8415i
  0.5403 + 0.8415i   -0.4161 + 0.9093i   -0.9900 + 0.1411i

>> exp(Z1)

ans =

  2.7183  2.7183  7.3891
 20.0855  7.3891  0.3679
  2.7183  7.3891 20.0855
```

(*continued*)

Function	Meaning
log (Z)	*Base e logarithm of Z.*

```
>> log(Z)

ans =

0.3466 - 0.7854i   0.3466 + 0.7854i   0.6931 + 1.5708i
1.9033 - 1.1071i   1.4979 + 1.1071i        0 - 1.5708i
0       + 1.5708i   0.6931 + 1.5708i   1.0986 + 1.5708i

>> log(Z1)

ans =

     0                  0              0.6931
1.0986 0.6931        0 + 3.1416i          ˙
     0 0.6931                         1.0986
```

log10 (Z)	*Base 10 logarithm of Z.*

```
>> log10(Z)

ans =

0.1505 - 0.3411i   0.1505 + 0.3411i   0.3010 + 0.6822i
0.8266 - 0.4808i   0.6505 + 0.4808i        0 - 0.6822i
0       + 0.6822i   0.3010 + 0.6822i   0.4771 + 0.6822i

>> log10(Z1)

ans =

     0                  0              0.3010
0.4771 0.3010        0 + 1.3644i
     0                0.3010          0.4771
```

(*continued*)

Function	Meaning
log2 (Z)	*Base 2 logarithm of Z.*

```
>> log2(Z)

ans =

0.5000 - 1.1331i    0.5000 + 1.1331i    1.0000 + 2.2662i
2.7459 - 1.5973i    2.1610 + 1.5973i         0 - 2.2662i
0       + 2.2662i    1.0000 + 2.2662i    1.5850 + 2.2662i
>> log2(Z1)

ans =

     0                  0              1.0000
1.5850 1.0000           0 + 4.5324i
     0 1.0000                         1.5850
```

Function	Meaning
pow2 (Z)	*Base 2 exponential function (2^Z).*

```
>> pow2(Z)

ans =

 1.5385 - 1.2779i    1.5385 + 1.2779i    0.1835 + 0.9830i
-4.2054 + 6.8055i   -3.7307 + 1.4427i    0.7692 - 0.6390i
 0.7692 + 0.6390i    0.1835 + 0.9830i   -0.4870 + 0.8734i

>> pow2(Z1)

ans =

2.0000 2.0000 4.0000
8.0000 4.0000 0.5000
2.0000 4.0000 8.0000
```

(continued)

196

Function	Meaning
sqrt (Z)	*Square root of Z.*

```
>> sqrt (Z)

ans =

1.0987 - 0.4551i    1.0987 + 0.4551i    1.0000 + 1.0000i
2.2032 - 1.3617i    1.7989 + 1.1118i    0.7071 - 0.7071i
0.7071 + 0.7071i    1.0000 + 1.0000i    1.2247 + 1.2247i

>> sqrt(Z1)

ans =

1.0000 1.0000 1.4142
1.7321 1.4142 0 + 1.0000i
1.0000 1.4142 1.7321
```

5.5.4 Specific Features of Complex Matrices

MATLAB incorporates a specific group of functions of a complex variable allowing you to work with moduli, arguments, and real and imaginary parts. Among these functions are the following:

Function	Meaning
abs (Z)	*The complex modulus (absolute value).*

```
>> abs (Z)

ans =

    1.4142    1.4142    2.0000
    6.7082    4.4721    1.0000
    1.0000    2.0000    3.0000

>> abs(Z1)

ans =

    1 1 2
    3-2-1
    1 2 3
```

angle (Z)	*Argument function.*

```
>> angle (Z)

ans =

   -0.7854    0.7854    1.5708
   -1.1071    1.1071   -1.5708
    1.5708    1.5708    1.5708

>> angle(Z1)

ans =

    0         0         0
    0         0      3.1416
    0         0         0
```

(continued)

Function	Meaning
conj (Z)	*Complex conjugate.*

```
>> conj (Z)

ans =

1.0000 + 1.0000i   1.0000 - 1.0000i      0 - 2.0000i
3.0000 + 6.0000i   2.0000 - 4.0000i      0 + 1.0000i
        0 - 1.0000i         0 - 2.0000i      0 - 3.0000i

>> conj(Z1)

ans =

1 1 2
2-3-1
1 2 3
```

real (Z)	*Real part.*

```
>> real (Z)

ans =

1     1     0
3     2     0
0     0     0

>> real(Z1)

ans =

1 1 2
2-3-1
1 2 3
```

(continued)

199

Function	Meaning
imag (Z)	*Imaginary part.*

```
>> imag (Z)

ans =

-1 1 2
-4 6 -1
 1 2 3

>> imag (Z1)

ans =

0 0 0
0 0 0
0 0 0
```

floor (Z)	*Floor function applied to real and imaginary parts.*

```
>> floor(12.357*Z)

ans =

12.0000 -13.0000i   12.0000 +12.0000i       0 +24.0000i
37.0000 -75.0000i   24.0000 +49.0000i       0 -13.0000i
      0 +12.0000i         0 +24.0000i       0 +37.0000i

>> floor(12.357*Z1)

ans =

12   12   24
37   24  -13
12  -24  -37
```

(*continued*)

Function	Meaning
ceil (Z)	*Ceiling function applied to real and imaginary parts.*

```
>> ceil(12.357*Z)

ans =

13.0000 - 12.0000i   13.0000 + 13.0000i        0 + 25.0000i
38.0000 - 74.0000i   25.0000 + 50.0000i        0 - 12.0000i
       0 + 13.0000i         0 + 25.0000i        0 + 38.0000i

>> ceil(12.357*Z1)

ans =

13 13   25
38 25  -12
13 25   38
```

round (Z)	*Round function applied to real and imaginary parts.*

```
>> round(12.357*Z)

ans =

12.0000 - 12.0000i   12.0000 + 12.0000i        0 + 25.0000i
37.0000 - 74.0000i   25.0000 + 49.0000i        0 - 12.0000i
       0 + 12.0000i         0 + 25.0000i        0 + 37.0000i

>> round(12.357*Z1)

ans =

12 -12 -25
37  25 -12
12  25  37
```

(*continued*)

Function	Meaning
fix (Z)	*Fix applied to real and imaginary parts.*

```
>> fix(12.357*Z)

ans =

12.0000 - 12.0000i   12.0000 + 12.0000i        0 + 24.0000i
37.0000 - 74.0000i   24.0000 + 49.0000i        0 - 12.0000i
       0 + 12.0000i          0 + 24.0000i        0 + 37.0000i

>> fix(12.357*Z1)

ans =

12   12   24
24  -37   12
12  -24  -37
```

5.6 Operations with Real and Complex Variables

MATLAB includes the usual matrix operations of sum, difference, product, exponentiation and inversion. Obviously all these operations will also be valid for real matrices. The following table summarizes those operations that are valid both for numerical and algebraic real and complex matrices.

A + B   *Sum of matrices.*

```
>> A=[1+i, 1-i, 2i; -i,-3i,6-5i; 2+3i, 2-3i, i]

A =

   1.0000 + 1.0000i    1.0000 - 1.0000i        0 + 2.0000i
        0 - 1.0000i         0 - 3.0000i   6.0000 - 5.0000i
   2.0000 + 3.0000i    2.0000 - 3.0000i        0 + 1.0000i

>> B=[i, -i, 2i; 1-i,7-3i,2-5i; 8-6i, 5-i, 1+i]

B =

        0 + 1.0000i         0 - 1.0000i        0 + 2.0000i
   1.0000 - 1.0000i    7.0000 - 3.0000i   2.0000 - 5.0000i
   8.0000 - 6.0000i    5.0000 - 1.0000i   1.0000 + 1.0000i

>> A1=[1 6 2; 3 5 0; 2 4 -1]

A1 =

   1     6     2
   3     5     0
   2     4    -1

>> B1=[-3 -6 1; -3 -5 2; 12 14 -10]

B1 =

   -3    -6     1
   -3    -5     2
   12    14   -10

>> A+B

ans =

    1.0000 + 2.0000i    1.0000 - 2.0000i        0 +  4.0000i
    1.0000 - 2.0000i    7.0000 - 6.0000i   8.0000 - 10.0000i
   10.0000 - 3.0000i    7.0000 - 4.0000i   1.0000 +  2.0000i

>> A1+B1

ans =

   -2     0     3
    0     0     2
   14    18   -11
```

(*continued*)

A-B   *Difference of matrices.*

```
>> A-B

ans =

  1.0000                 1.0000                  0
 -1.0000                -7.0000              4.0000
 -6.0000 + 9.0000i  -3.0000 - 2.0000i  -1.0000

>> A1-B1

ans =

   4     12     1
   6     10    -2
 -10    -10     9
```

A * B   *Product of matrices.*

```
>> A * B

ans =

 11.0000 + 15.0000i    7.0000 -  1.0000i  - 7.0000 -  3.0000i
 16.0000 - 79.0000i   15.0000 - 52.0000i  - 2.0000 -  5.0000i
  2.0000 +  5.0000i    9.0000 - 24.0000i - 18.0000 - 11.0000i

>> A1*B1

ans =

   3     -8     -7
 -24    -43     13
 -30    -46     20
```

(*continued*)

A^n   *nth power of the matrix A.*

>> A^3

ans =

1.0e+002 *

0.1000 - 0.3400i -0.3200 - 0.1200i   0.3400 - 0.3600i
0.0900 - 0.0300i -1.0700 + 0.2100i -2.2500 - 0.6700i
0.3700 - 0.7900i -1.0300 - 0.0300i -0.0700 - 0.3700i

>> A1^3

ans =

155   358   46
159   347   30
106   232   19

ans =

Columns 1 through 2

1.0000 - 1.0000i   2.0000

Columns 3 through 4

6.0000 - 10. 0000i 60.0000 + 36 0000i

>> cumprod ([1, 0, -23, 12, 16])

ans =

1   0   0   0   0

(*continued*)

P^A   *Scalar p raised to the power of the matrix A.*

```
>> 3^A

ans =


   0.0159 - 1.2801i   -0.5297 + 2.8779i   -1.9855 + 3.0796i
 -10.3372 + 0.4829i   17.0229 +12.9445i   14.7327 +20.1633i
  -5.0438 + 0.2388i    7.0696 + 6.9611i    5.7189 + 9.5696i

>> 3^A1

ans =

1.0e+003 *

2.2230    4.9342    0.4889
2.1519    4.7769    0.4728
1.4346    3.1844    0.3156
```

A'   *Transpose of the matrix A.*

```
>> A'

ans =

1.0000 - 1.0000i        0 + 1.0000i   2.0000 - 3.0000i
1.0000 + 1.0000i        0 + 3.0000i   2.0000 + 3.0000i
       0 - 2.0000i   6.0000 + 5.0000i        0 - 1.0000i

>> A1'

ans =

1    3    2
6    5    4
2    0   -1
```

(*continued*)

A^-1   *Inverse of A .*

```
>> A^-1

ans =

-2.5000 + 2.0000i  -0.0500 + 0.6500i   0.8500 - 1.0500i
 0.5000 + 3.0000i   0.5500 + 0.3500i  -0.3500 - 0.9500i
-1.0000 - 1.0000i  -0.2000 + 0.1000i   0.4000 + 0.3000i

>> A1^-1

ans =

-0.2941     0.8235   -0.5882
 0.1765    -0.2941    0.3529
 0.1176     0.4706   -0.7647

>> A*A^-1

ans =

 1.0000              0.0000 - 0.0000i  -0.0000 + 0.0000i
-0.0000 - 0.0000i    1.0000 + 0.0000i   0.0000
 0.0000 + 0.0000i    0.0000             1.0000 + 0.0000i

>> A1*A1^-1

ans =

 1.0000    -0.0000         0
-0.0000     1.0000         0
-0.0000    -0.0000    1.0000
```

(continued)

A\B   *If A is square A\B= (A-1) * B and if A is not square A\B is the solution in the sense of least-squares of the system AX = B.*

```
>> A\B

ans =

 -0.9000 -15.3000i    6.8000 + 1.1000i    1.0500 - 3.6500i
-10.6000 -  5.2000i    5.2000 - 4.1000i   -2.5500 - 2.3500i
  5.9000    0.7000i    0.2000 + 3.4000i    2.2000 - 0.1000i

>> A1\B1

ans =

 -8.6471 -10.5882   7.2353
  4.5882   5.3529  -3.9412
-10.9412 -13.7647   8.7059
```

(*continued*)

B/A   *Equivalent to A'\B'*

```
>> B/A

ans =


 3.0000 - 5.0000i   -0.5000 - 1.0000i   -0.5000 + 2.0000i
 5.0000 + 27.0000i    5.6000 + 2.7000i   -3.2000 - 8.9000i
-2.5000 + 43.5000i    6.3000 + 6.6000i   -2.1000 -17.2000i


>> A'\B'

ans =


3.0000 + 5.0000i    5.0000 -27.0000i   -2.5000 -43.5000i
-0.5000 + 1.0000i    5.6000 - 2.7000i    6.3000 - 6.6000i
-0.5000 - 2.0000i   -3.2000 + 8.9000i   -2.1000 +17.2000i


>> B1/A1

ans =


-0.0588    -0.2353    -1.1176
 0.2353    -0.0588    -1.5294
-2.2353     1.0588     5.5294


>> A1'\B1'

ans =


-0.0588     0.2353    -2.2353
-0.2353    -0.0588     1.0588
-1.1176    -1.5294     5.5294
```

EXERCISE 5-1

Given the complex numbers $z_1 = 1-i$, and $z_2 = 5i$, calculate: z_1^3 z_1^2/z_2^4, $z_1^{1/2}$, $z_2^{3/2}$, $\ln(z_1+z_2)$, $sin(z_1-z_2)$, and tanh (z_1/z_2).

```
>> Z1=1-i

Z1 =

   1.0000 - 1.0000i

>> Z2=5i

Z2 =

        0 + 5.0000i

>> Z1^3

ans =

  -2.0000 - 2.0000i

>> Z1^2/Z2^4

ans =

        0 - 0.0032i

>> sqrt(Z1)

ans =

   1.0987 - 0.4551i

>> sqrt(Z2^3)

ans =

   7.9057 - 7.9057i

>> log(Z1+Z2)

ans =

   1.4166 + 1.3258i
```

```
>> sin(Z1-Z2)

ans =

  1.6974e+002 -1.0899e+002i

>> tanh(Z1/Z2)

ans =

  -0.2052 - 0.1945i
```

EXERCISE 5-2

Perform the following operations with complex numbers:

$$\frac{i^8 - i^{-8}}{3 - 4i} + 1, i^{\sin(1+i)}, (2 + \ln(i))^{1/i}, (1+i)^i, i^{\ln(1+i)}, (1 + \sqrt{3}i)^{1-i}$$

```
>> (i^8-i^(-8))/(3-4*i) + 1

ans =

    1

>> i^(sin(1+i))

ans =

 -0.16665202215166 + 0.329041394503071i

>> (2+log(i))^(1/i)

ans =

  1.15809185259777 - 1.563880539890231i

>> (1+i)^i

ans =

  0.42882900629437 + 0.154871752464251i

>> i^(log(1+i))
```

ans =

  0.24911518828716 + 0.150819744484717i

>> (1+sqrt(3)*i)^(1-i)

ans =

  5.34581479196611 + 1.975948834528 73i

EXERCISE 5-3

Find the real part, imaginary part, modulus and argument of the following expressions:

$$i^{3+i}, (1+\sqrt{3}\,i)^{1-i}, i^{i^i}, i^i$$

>> Z1=i^3*i; Z2=(1+sqrt(3)*i)^(1-i); Z3=(i^i)^i;Z4=i^i;

>> format short

>> real([Z1 Z2 Z3 Z4])

ans =

    1.0000   5.3458   0.0000   0.2079

>> imag([Z1 Z2 Z3 Z4])

ans =

         0   1.9759   -1.0000   0

>> abs([Z1 Z2 Z3 Z4])

ans =

    1.0000   5.6993   1.0000   0.2079

>> angle([Z1 Z2 Z3 Z4])

ans =

         0   0.3541   -1.5708   0

EXERCISE 5-4

Consider the 3×3 matrix *M* whose elements are the squares of the first nine positive integers, multiplied by the imaginary unit (reading from left to right and top to bottom).

Find the square, the square root and the exponential to base 2 and − 2 of *M*.

Find the elementwise Naperian logarithm and base e exponential of *M*.

Find e^M and *log(M)*.

```
>> M=i*[1 2 3;4 5 6;7 8 9]

M =

        0 + 1.0000i        0 + 2.0000i        0 + 3.0000i
        0 + 4.0000i        0 + 5.0000i        0 + 6.0000i
        0 + 7.0000i        0 + 8.0000i        0 + 9.0000i

>> C=M^2

C =

   -30    -36    -42
   -66    -81    -96
  -102   -126   -150

>> D=M^(1/2)

D =

   0.8570 - 0.2210i   0.5370 + 0.2445i   0.2169 + 0.7101i
   0.7797 + 0.6607i   0.9011 + 0.8688i   1.0224 + 1.0769i
   0.7024 + 1.5424i   1.2651 + 1.4930i   1.8279 + 1.4437i

>> 2^M

ans =

   0.7020 - 0.6146i  -0.1693 - 0.2723i  -0.0407 + 0.0699i
  -0.2320 - 0.3055i   0.7366 - 0.3220i  -0.2947 - 0.3386i
  -0.1661 + 0.0036i  -0.3574 - 0.3717i   0.4513 - 0.7471i

>> (-2)^M

ans =

   17.3946 - 16.8443i    4.3404 - 4.5696i   -7.7139 + 7.7050i
    1.5685 - 1.8595i     1.1826 - 0.5045i   -1.2033 + 0.8506i
  -13.2575 + 13.1252i   -3.9751 + 3.5607i    6.3073 - 6.0038i
```

```
>> log(M)

ans =

        0 + 1.5708i    0.6931 + 1.5708i    1.0986 + 1.5708i
   1.3863 + 1.5708i    1.6094 + 1.5708i    1.7918 + 1.5708i
   1.9459 + 1.5708i    2.0794 + 1.5708i    2.1972 + 1.5708i

>> exp(M)

ans =

   0.5403 + 0.8415i   -0.4161 + 0.9093i   -0.9900 + 0.1411i
  -0.6536 - 0.7568i    0.2837 - 0.9589i    0.9602 - 0.2794i
   0.7539 + 0.6570i   -0.1455 + 0.9894i   -0.9111 + 0.4121i

>> logm(M)

ans =

   -5.4033 - 0.8472i   11.9931 - 0.3109i   -5.3770 + 0.8846i
   12.3029 + 0.0537i  -22.3087 + 0.8953i   12.6127 + 0.4183i
   -4.7574 + 1.6138i   12.9225 + 0.7828i   -4.1641 + 0.6112i

>> expm(M)

ans =

   0.3802 - 0.6928i   -0.3738 - 0.2306i   -0.1278 + 0.2316i
  -0.5312 - 0.1724i    0.3901 - 0.1434i   -0.6886 - 0.1143i
  -0.4426 + 0.3479i   -0.8460 - 0.0561i   -0.2493 - 0.4602i
```

EXERCISE 5-5

Consider the vector sum Z of the complex vector $V = (i, -i, i)$ and the real vector $R = (0, 1, 1)$. Find the mean, median, standard deviation, variance, sum, product, maximum and minimum of the elements of V, as well as its gradient, the discrete Fourier transform and its inverse.

```
>> Z=[i,-i,i]

Z =

      0 + 1.0000i       0 - 1.0000i       0 + 1.0000i
```

```
>> R=[0,1,1]

R =

     0    1    1

>> V=Z+R

V =

      0 + 1.0000i    1.0000 - 1.0000i    1.0000 + 1.0000i

>> [mean(V),median(V),std(V),var(V),sum(V),prod(V),max(V),min(V)]'

ans =

   0.6667 - 0.3333i
   1.0000 + 1.0000i
   1.2910
   1.6667
   2.0000 - 1.0000i
        0 - 2.0000i
   1.0000 + 1.0000i
        0 - 1.0000i

>> gradient(V)

ans =

   1.0000 - 2.0000i   0.5000                    0 + 2.0000i

>> fft(V)

ans =

   2.0000 + 1.0000i  -2.7321 + 1.0000i   0.7321 + 1.0000i

>> ifft(V)

ans =

   0.6667 + 0.3333i   0.2440 + 0.3333i  -0.9107 + 0.3333i
```

EXERCISE 5-6

Given the following matrices:

$$A1 = \begin{bmatrix} 1 & 0 & 0 \\ 0 & 1 & 0 \\ 0 & 0 & 1 \end{bmatrix} \quad A2 = \begin{bmatrix} 0 & 1 & 0 \\ 0 & 0 & 1 \\ 0 & 0 & 0 \end{bmatrix} \quad B1 = \begin{bmatrix} 0 & 1 & 2 \\ 0 & -1 & 3 \\ 0 & 0 & 0 \end{bmatrix} \quad B2 = \begin{bmatrix} -i & i & -i \\ 0 & 0 & i \\ 0 & 0 & i \end{bmatrix}$$

$$C1 = \begin{bmatrix} 1 & -1 & 0 \\ -1 & sqrt(2)i & -sqrt(2)i \\ 0 & 0 & -1 \end{bmatrix} \quad C2 = \begin{bmatrix} 0 & 2 & 1 \\ 1 & 0 & 0 \\ 1 & -1 & 0 \end{bmatrix}$$

First calculate $A1 + A2$, $B1$-$B2$ and $C1 + C2$.

Then calculate AB - BA, $A^2 + B^2 + C^2$, ABC, $sqrt(A) + sqrt(B)$ - $sqrt(C)$, $(e^B + e^C)$, their transposes and their inverses.

Finally check that any matrix multiplied by its inverse yields the identity matrix

```
>> A1=eye(3)

A1 =

     1     0     0
     0     1     0
     0     0     1

>> A2=[0 1 0; 0 0 1;0 0 0]

A2 =

     0     1     0
     0     0     1
     0     0     0

>> A= A1+A2

A =

     1     1     0
     0     1     1
     0     0     1
```

```
>> B1=[0 1 2;0 -1 3;0 0 0]

B1 =

    0    1    2
    0   -1    3
    0    0    0

>> B2=[-i i -i;0 0 i;0 0 i]



B2 =

    0 - 1.0000i      0 + 1.0000i      0 - 1.0000i
    0                0                0 + 1.0000i
    0                0                0 + 1.0000i

>> B=B1-B2

B =

    0 + 1.0000i   1.0000 - 1.0000i   2.0000 + 1.0000i
    0                    -1.0000      3.0000 - 1.0000i
    0                     0                0 - 1.0000i

>> C1=[1, -1, 0;-1,sqrt(2)*i,-sqrt(2)*i;0,0,-1]

C1 =

   1.0000             -1.0000                 0
  -1.0000              0 + 1.4142i      0 - 1.4142i
        0              0                   -1.0000

>> C2=[0 2 1;1 0 0;1 -1 0]

C2 =

    0    2    1
    1    0    0
    1   -1    0

>> C=C1+C2

C =

   1.0000            1.0000            1.0000
        0            0 + 1.4142i       0 - 1.4142i
   1.0000           -1.0000           -1.0000
```

```
>> M1=A*B-B*A

M1 =

        0           -1.0000 - 1.0000i    2.0000
        0                 0              1.0000 - 1.0000i
        0                 0                    0

>> M2=A^2+B^2+C^2

M2 =

   2.0000              2.0000 + 3.4142i    3.0000 - 5.4142i
        0 - 1.4142i   -0.0000 + 1.4142i    0.0000 - 0.5858i
        0              2.0000 - 1.4142i    2.0000 + 1.4142i

>> M3=A*B*C

M3 =

   5.0000 + 1.0000i   -3.5858 + 1.0000i   -6.4142 + 1.0000i
   3.0000 - 2.0000i   -3.0000 + 0.5858i   -3.0000 + 3.4142i
        0 - 1.0000i         0 + 1.0000i         0 + 1.0000i

>> M4=sqrtm(A)+sqrtm(B)-sqrtm(C)

M4 =

   0.6356 + 0.8361i   -0.3250 - 0.8204i    3.0734 + 1.2896i
   0.1582 - 0.1521i    0.0896 + 0.5702i    3.3029 - 1.8025i
  -0.3740 - 0.2654i    0.7472 + 0.3370i    1.2255 + 0.1048i


>> M5=expm(A)*(expm(B)+expm(C))

M5 =

  14.1906 - 0.0822i    5.4400 + 4.2724i   17.9169 - 9.5842i
   4.5854 - 1.4972i    0.6830 + 2.1575i    8.5597 - 7.6573i
   3.5528 + 0.3560i    0.1008 - 0.7488i    3.2433 - 1.8406i

>> inv(A)

ans =

    1    -1     1
    0     1    -1
    0     0     1
```

```
>> inv(B)

ans =

        0 - 1.0000i   -1.0000 - 1.0000i   -4.0000 + 3.0000i
        0                  -1.0000          1.0000 + 3.0000i
        0                      0                 0 + 1.0000i

>> inv(C)

ans =

   0.5000                   0              0.5000
   0.2500              0 - 0.3536i        -0.2500
   0.2500              0 + 0.3536i        -0.2500

>> [A*inv(A) B*inv(B) C*inv(C)]

ans =

    1    0    0    1    0    0    1    0    0
    0    1    0    0    1    0    0    1    0
    0    0    1    0    0    1    0    0    1

>> A'

ans =

    1    0    0
    1    1    0
    0    1    1

>> B'

ans =

        0 - 1.0000i          0                   0
   1.0000 + 1.0000i     -1.0000                  0
   2.0000 - 1.0000i    3.0000 + 1.0000i     0 + 1.0000i

>> C'

ans =

   1.0000                   0              1.0000
   1.0000              0 - 1.4142i        -1.0000
   1.0000              0 + 1.4142i        -1.0000
```

EXERCISE 5-7

Apply the sine, base e exponential, logarithm, square root, modulus, argument and rounding functions to each of the following matrices:

$$A = \begin{bmatrix} 1 & 2 & 3 \\ 4 & 5 & 6 \\ 7 & 8 & 9 \end{bmatrix}, \quad B = \begin{bmatrix} 1+i & 2+i \\ 3+i & 4+i \end{bmatrix}.$$

Calculate e^B and $ln(A)$.

```
>> A=[1 2 3; 4 5 6; 7 8 9]

A =

    1    2    3
    4    5    6
    7    8    9

>> sin(A)

ans =

    0.8415    0.9093    0.1411
   -0.7568   -0.9589   -0.2794
    0.6570    0.9894    0.4121

>> B=[1+i 2+i;3+i,4+i]

B =

   1.0000 + 1.0000i   2.0000 + 1.0000i
   3.0000 + 1.0000i   4.0000 + 1.0000i

>> sin(B)

ans =

   1.2985 + 0.6350i   1.4031 - 0.4891i
   0.2178 - 1.1634i  -1.1678 - 0.7682i

>> exp(A)

ans =

   1.0e+003 *

    0.0027    0.0074    0.0201
    0.0546    0.1484    0.4034
    1.0966    2.9810    8.1031
```

```
>> exp(B)

ans =

    1.4687 +  2.2874i   3.9923 +  6.2177i
   10.8523 + 16.9014i  29.4995 + 45.9428i

>> log(B)

ans =

   0.3466 + 0.7854i   0.8047 + 0.4636i
   1.1513 + 0.3218i   1.4166 + 0.2450i

>> sqrt(B)

ans =

   1.0987 + 0.4551i   1.4553 + 0.3436i
   1.7553 + 0.2848i   2.0153 + 0.2481i

>> abs(B)

ans =

    1.4142    2.2361
    3.1623    4.1231

>> imag(B)

ans =

    1    1
    1    1

>> fix(sin(B))

ans =

   1.0000            1.0000
   0 - 1.0000i  -    1.0000

>> ceil(log(A))

ans =

    0    1    2
    2    2    2
    2    3    3
```

```
>> sign(B)

ans =

   0.7071 + 0.7071i   0.8944 + 0.4472i
   0.9487 + 0.3162i   0.9701 + 0.2425i
```

The exponential functions, square root and logarithm used above apply element to element to the array, and have nothing to do with the matrix exponential and logarithmic functions that are used below.

```
>> expm(B)

ans =

  1.0e+002 *

  -0.3071 + 0.4625i   -0.3583 + 0.6939i
  -0.3629 + 1.0431i   -0.3207 + 1.5102i

>> logm(A)

ans =

  -5.6588 + 2.7896i   12.5041 - 0.4325i   -5.6325 - 0.5129i
  12.8139 - 0.7970i  -23.3307 + 2.1623i   13.1237 - 1.1616i
  -5.0129 - 1.2421i   13.4334 - 1.5262i   -4.4196 + 1.3313i
```

EXERCISE 5-8

Solve the following equation in the complex field:

sin (z) = 2.

```
>> vpa (solve ('sin (z) = 2'))

ans =

 1.3169578969248167086250463473308 * i + 1.5707963267948966192313216916398
 1.5707963267948966192313216916398 1.3169578969248167086250463473308 * i
```

EXERCISE 5-9

Solve the following equations:

a. $1+x+x^2+x^3+x^4+x^5 = 0$

b. $x^2+(6-i)x+8-4i = 0$

c. $\tan(Z) = 3i/5$

```
>> solve('1+x+x^2+x^3+x^4+x^5 = 0')

ans =

                    -1
 -1/2 - (3-^(1/2) * i) / 2
  1/2 - (3-^(1/2) * i) / 2
 -1/2 + (3 ^(1/2) * i) / 2
  1/2 + (3 ^(1/2) * i) / 2

>> solve ('x ^ 2 +(6-i) * x + 8-4 * i = 0')

ans =

    -4
 i 2

>> vpa (solve ('tan (Z) = 3 * i/5 '))

ans =

0.69314718055994530941723212145818 * i
```

EXERCISE 5-10

Find the results of the following operations:

a. the fourth root of - 1 and 1;

b. the fifth roots of 2 + 2i and - 1 + i√3;

c. the real part of tan (iLn ((a+ib) / (a-ib)));

d. the imaginary part of $(2 + i)^{cos(4+i)}$.

```
>> solve('x^4+1=0')

ans =

 2 ^(1/2) *(-i/2-1/2)
 2 ^(1/2) *(i/2-1/2)
 2 ^(1/2) *(1/2-i/2)
 2 ^(1/2) *(i/2 + 1/2)

>> pretty (solve('x^4+1=0'))

   +-                  -+
   |    1/2 / i 1 \ |
   |   2    | - - - - |  |
   |        \   2   2 /  |
   |                     |
   |    1/2 / i 1 \ |
   |   2    | - - - |   |
   |        \ 2   2 /   |
   |                     |
   |    1/2 / 1 i \ |
   |   2    | - - - |   |
   |        \ 2   2 /   |
   |                     |
   |    1/2 / i 1 \ |
   |   2    | - + - |   |
   |        \ 2   2 /   |
   +-                  -+

>> solve('x^4-1=0')

ans =

 -1
  1
 -i
  i

>> vpa(solve('x^5-2-2*i=0'))
```

ans =

     0.19259341768888084906125263406469 * i + 1.2159869826496146992458377919696
    -0.87055056329612413913627001747975 * i - 0.87055056329612413913627001747975
     0.55892786746600970394985946846702 * i - 1.0969577045083811131206798770216
     0.55892786746600970394985946846702   1.0969577045083811131206798770216 * i
     1.2159869826496146992458377919696 * i + 0.19259341768888084906125263406469

>> vpa(solve('x^5+1-sqrt(3)*i=0'))

ans =

     0.46721771281818786757419290603946 * i + 1.0493881644090691705137652947201
     1.1424056652180689506550734259384 * i - 0.12007167380592154112409047542 85
     0.76862922680258900220179378744147   0.85364923855044142809268986292246 * i
    -0.99480195671282768870147766609475 * i - 0.57434917749851750339931347338896
     0.23882781722701229856490119703938 * i - 1.1235965399072191281921551333441

>> simplify (vpa (real (tan (i * log ((a+i*b) /(a-i*b)))))))

ans =

-0.5 * tanh (conj (log ((a^2 + 2.0*a*b*i-1.0*b^2) /(a^2 + b^2))) * i + (0.5 * ((a^2 +
2.0*a*b*i-1.0*b^2) ^ 2 /(a^2 + b^2) ^ 2 - 1) * i) / ((a^2 + 2.0*a*b*i-1.0*b^2) ^ 2 /(a^2 +
b^2) ^ 2 + 1))

>> simplify(vpa(imag((2+i)^cos(4-i))))

ans =

-0.62107490808037524310236676683417

Get the eBook for only $10!

Now you can take the weightless companion with you anywhere, anytime. Your purchase of this book entitles you to 3 electronic versions for only $10.

This Apress title will prove so indispensible that you'll want to carry it with you everywhere, which is why we are offering the eBook in **3 formats** for only $10 if you have already purchased the print book.

Convenient and fully searchable, the PDF version enables you to easily find and copy code—or perform examples by quickly toggling between instructions and applications. The MOBI format is ideal for your Kindle, while the ePUB can be utilized on a variety of mobile devices.

Go to www.apress.com/promo/tendollars to purchase your companion eBook.

Apress®
THE EXPERT'S VOICE™